Ra

Acc. N

BENÍTEZ

Rafa
BENÍTEZ

WITHDRAWN FROM STOCK

●◆ Paco Lloret

dewi lewis media ltd

Rafa BENÍTEZ
By Paco Lloret

This edition first published in the UK in September 2005 by
Dewi Lewis Media Ltd
8, Broomfield Road
Heaton Moor
Stockport SK4 4ND
www.dewilewismedia.com

> Originally published in Spain by
Engloba Edicíon, Valencia

> Photographs
© Getty Images, Paco Martí, Valencia CF and Liverpool FC Press Office
and the Benítez-Maudes family

> Iberian Football Consultant for this edition
Adam Gumbley

> Translation
Malcolm Marsh

> Original Design Concept
Arco da Velha – Design e Ilustração, Lda, Portugal. Based on the design
originally conceived for the book 'José Mourinho: Made in Portugal'

> Artwork Production
Dewi Lewis Media Ltd

> Print and binding
Biddles Ltd, Kings Lynn

ISBN: 0-9546843-7-0

12   11   10   9   8   7   6   5   4   3   2   1

>> **CONTENTS**

INTRODUCTION

RAFA BENÍTEZ

❧ Adam Gumbley

INTRODUCTION

The Atatürk Olympic Stadium, Istanbul, approximately 10.35pm local time on Wednesday 25th May 2005. Liverpool Football Club are on the brink of outright humiliation in the UEFA Champions League final. For Rafael Benítez, the next fifteen minutes represent the most important halftime team talk of a coaching career that began almost two decades ago. As he surveys the forlorn and despondent young men in front of him, Benítez somehow succeeds in summoning reserves of courage and a sense of pride in the famous red shirt. Mixed with the emotion, and true to his style of remaining calm under pressure, the Liverpool manager displays astute tactical awareness in introducing Dietmar Hamann for the start of the second half. The substitution liberates Steven Gerrard and the captain finds sufficient space in the Milan area to score the crucial opening goal. Within fifteen minutes of the restart, Liverpool are back on level terms after the most extraordinary seven-minute spell in the history of the great competition. After two hours of an epic encounter, goalkeeper Jerzy Dudek emerges as the unlikely hero following his astonishing save from Shevchenko and subsequent exploits in the penalty shoot-out.

In his first season at Anfield, Rafael Benítez has emulated the feats of his illustrious predecessors Bob Paisley and Joe Fagan. The first Spaniard to manage Liverpool, or indeed any English club, has achieved *la inmortalidad* by restoring the glory days and ensuring a replica of the famous old trophy will reside at Anfield for future generations to admire.

For Benítez, *that* night in Istanbul represented the culmination of many years of hard work and dedication – not even the great Bill Shankly had delivered European Cup success. And yet, as he took in the enormity of his achievement, he could have reflected that his professional life looked somewhat different less than a decade earlier. Following successive failures at the helm of Valladolid and Osasuna, the latter after less than a dozen matches in charge, Benítez faced the very real possibility of his embryonic managerial career coming to an end almost before it had truly begun. Another failure could see him doomed to relative obscurity for the rest of his professional life. Under pressure, he was granted the opportunity to resurrect his career with second division Extremadura, and duly delivered, leading them to promotion in his first season. Relegation followed the next season but Benítez returned to form with Tenerife, clinching the second division title for the Canary Islanders.

It was at this stage of his career that Benítez was offered his first real opportunity to shine. He was certainly not the first choice to manage Valencia, and there were many who questioned his coaching credentials at the time, but in his debut season he delivered the club's first title in thirty-one years. He had inherited a strong squad of players from Héctor Cúper, the majority of whom had far more experience of top flight football than him, but Benítez succeeded in moulding a collection of international superstars into a strong unit and in 2004 led Valencia to a league and UEFA Cup double and the most successful season in their 85-year history. Vindication for the Valencia board but after an acrimonious departure Benítez surpassed his achievement the following year by leading Liverpool to the summit of European football. A remarkable two-year period on a personal level as Benítez equalled the feat of the only other man to win the UEFA Cup and Champions League in successive seasons: a certain José Mourinho.

In many ways there are remarkable similarities between the two young coaches from the Iberian peninsular and perhaps together they represent a new breed of football manager for the 21st century. However, whereas Mourinho enjoyed almost immediate success with Chelsea, it took time for Benítez to make his mark, as the Merseysiders slumped to fourteen league defeats and finished thirty-seven points behind the eventual champions. His appointment as Liverpool manager was generally welcomed by the fans, but not even the most wildly optimistic *Kopite* could have envisaged what the latter stages of that first year held in store. The 2004-05 season was to be viewed as a period of transition as the *Reds* looked to move on from the Houllier era. Indeed, Liverpool's great European adventure almost came to an end at the first hurdle as they stumbled to a 2-1 aggregate victory over AK Graz in the qualifying round. Worse was to follow, in a bleak mid-winter period, Benítez and the faith he places in the rotation system were tested to the limit after successive defeats to Burnley in the FA Cup and to Manchester United and Southampton in the league.

Like his Portuguese counterpart however, Benítez failed to make the grade as a professional at the highest level, and his career was cut short by injury at the age of 26. Both men had the foresight to study for a qualification in Physical Education and both had the fortune to learn the intricacies of management from an experienced mentor, Benítez teaming up briefly with Vicente Del Bosque during his managerial tutelage at Real Madrid. The traditional view was that only those who had played the game at the highest level could go on to succeed in management. Yet perhaps, as Mourinho himself has commented, those with time to spare in their twenties and thirties are given a head start in assimilating the necessary knowledge and coaching techniques to succeed in the modern game. Indeed, between his spells in the Spanish lower leagues, the scholarly interest that Benítez takes in the work of other coaches resulted in a sabbatical year split between Italy and England. There, he diligently studied the techniques of modern managerial greats such as Marcello Lippi, Fabio Capello and Sir Alex Ferguson, before returning to Spain eager to put his new theories into practice.

This relentless thirst for knowledge and his legendary attention to detail is at the heart of the success that the Liverpool manager has enjoyed since he began his coaching career in 1986 with the Real Madrid youth side. The 'loner with the laptop', a phrase that Benítez himself once coined to describe his obsessive devotion to the game and love of his work, is a voracious student with a sharp, analytical mind. The qualities he possesses are the same as those that he demands from the players under his stewardship: discipline, professionalism, dedication, meticulous preparation, diligence and courage. The same courage and strength of character that Benítez displayed in leaving Real Madrid in 1995, his boyhood team where he had spent almost half his life, when it became clear that his managerial destiny lay elsewhere. Equally, he possessed the belief and resilience to take on the top job and succeed at Valencia, in the face of the many dissenting voices within the club.

Despite his achievements over recent years, Benítez has maintained an unassuming modesty and relatively low profile. His low-key celebrations at the final whistle in Istanbul aptly demonstrated the humility and respect for the opponent that he demands of his players. As he told his Tenerife squad shortly after they clinched promotion to the first division:

"You must always maintain your dignity and not lose your composure, not even in moments of the greatest euphoria."

This is certainly where the similarities between Benítez and Mourinho end. In this respect, Benítez is the very antithesis of *the Special One*, but his mild-mannered demeanour and docile nature do not mean that Benítez is unwilling to be ruthless where the situation demands. At Valencia, he frequently clashed with some of the more colourful characters of the dressing room because they didn't share his work ethic. Even those who performed so valiantly in Istanbul, such as Smicer and Baros, found that their efforts were no guarantee of a place in the Liverpool of the future. Truly the *Rafa revolution* is in full swing.

As Benítez starts to build his empire at Anfield, fellow TV pundit and friend Paco Lloret is in a privileged position to look back on the key milestones in the Liverpool manager's life, focusing on the successes and failures of the early days, and culminating in that unforgettable night on the banks of the Bosphorus.

Adam Gumbley
August 2005

PROLOGUE

Some day this guy will be manager of Valencia and will make us champions."

I can't remember if those were my exact words to Paco – my friend Paco Lloret – but I do remember it as if it were yesterday. I was talking about another friend of mine, Rafa Benítez, who wanted to speak to Paco and ask him to record on VHS all the games he could that were going through the control room of Channel 9 Valencian Television. He'd already asked me to do the same at Telemadrid and Eurosport. Here was the man that all our friends described as "a scholar – a football freak". One day he would see all his commitment, hard work and, of course, talent come to fruition. And I was hoping it would be with my team, our team – Paco's, mine and, before long, Rafa's too! Valencia Football Club.

If I remember correctly I made the comment a few months before the famous final in which Valencia lost to Deportivo at the Bernabéu. Paco and I witnessed it – him pitchside and drenched by the torrential rain, me, more fortunate, in the stand.

That night, the final having eventually been rained off, we ended up having supper in the Asador Donostiarra at around 1.30 in the morning. I had arranged to meet Rafa, and we were analysing the match – or rather he was, I was just listening. I remember telling Paco that he should come as well, but work prevented him. And so, yet another delay in my two friends, Paco and Rafa, meeting. They'd seen each other on television, they'd even spoken on the phone, but they'd never met face to face. Never shaken hands... strange.

I met Paco in the 1980s. How young we were! We both worked for Antena 3 Radio – him in Valencia, me in Madrid. We talked on the phone, wrote features on the handball games in which the teams from our respective cities played each other, and gradually became friendly – without becoming close. Almost from the very beginning, from my first call as a company colleague, I confessed to Paco my passion as a Valencia fan and bemoaned my less than ideal location in Madrid. I remember he was surprised, and it amused him too.

Our dealings were routine, carried out in a friendly way and in a spirit of cooperation, that's all. Years later, Paco joined the newly formed Canal 9 Valencian Television and I joined Telemadrid – another coincidence! Or simply fate?

It would be tennis, and more specifically the magic of Wimbledon, that would bring us closer, and our incipient friendship began to grow and develop.

We had both been sent there by our respective television stations. Our job as reporters, with its long hours, prevented us from talking as much as we would have liked about our Valencia, but whenever we could we would find a moment or two. This was the summer of 1990, and it was then that our admiration, affection and, in short, our friendship took off and grew. We became very good friends. As a result of our friendship, other friendships have sprung up – with Yolanda, his wife, with my father, with his daughters, with my children, with other friends of ours. That's life, isn't it? What is certain is that Paco is one of my best friends and it's a friendship I'm proud of.

I met Rafa around the same time. Rafa was a promising coach of the up-and-coming players of Real Madrid. He was well-known for having been a good player whose career had been cut short by injury, a knee injury that was made worse partly because of him not wanting to let people down – very probably an act of youthful irresponsibility – and because the extent of the injury wasn't properly recognised. He played while injured, believing it to be something insignificant. But the doctor's diagnosis had been incorrect. This prevented him from reaching the top level to which he aspired, and he had to settle for the second division.

Rafa has always known what he wanted to be – a football coach. Those who knew him as a player say that for his team mates he was a coach on the pitch. By the time he was a young coach with the up-and-coming players of Real Madrid, he was revolutionary in his training methods, his working systems, and in his absolute control of all the factors that can influence play on and off the pitch. He was a football scholar – a phrase that has had a very bad press both in my profession, journalism, and amongst the footballing fraternity, which is very strange, and shows the resistance to change in both disciplines.

Very few know that it was Rafa – talking informally with journalists covering the daily news of Real Madrid's first team – who disclosed that there was a gem amongst the young Madrid players who'd come from Atlético. The name – Raúl. That's being on the ball, isn't it?

Rafa spent periods in Real's second team, and he had the chance to show how much real ability he had, and not only with the youth side, with Real Valladolid. Few know the effort he put into making a side like Valladolid competitive, a side which expected to play in the second division, but unexpectedly played in the first division. That's where he toughened up, and how well it served him later.

Then he had experiences with Osasuna, Extremadura and Tenerife before moving to Valencia and then on to Liverpool. It was during his time at Extremadura that he, at last, met Paco Lloret. After years of talking on the phone – almost working together at a distance – they could, at last, shake hands. Two of my friends who were now also becoming friends, independent of their relationship with me.

Before he arrived at Valencia I was able to enjoy my friendship with Rafa as a fellow television commentator. It was a time when the pressure was off after the experiences he had lived through at Extremadura – a good period in his personal life, but not so good in his professional life.

In the course of our friendship, Rafa and I have commentated on matches for Telemadrid, Eurosport and pay per view. Together with other colleagues we started a programme called Multifútbol, which achieved a dream we footballers always had – Rafa too – to put pictures to the back-to-back programmes on Sundays which radio stations in Spain do so brilliantly.

Rafa's signing for Valencia – very discretely managed and a secret even to his friends (I found out about it only through the press… Paco rang me to tell me of the rumour) – was to confirm my comment at the start of the prologue to this great book. It seemed that my prophecy about my friend Rafa had come true – the best possible dream for my happiness, and for that of my friend Paco Lloret, had come true.

It hadn't though, the best was yet to come.

There are two other statements I'll never forget. The first was at the height of the pre-season of the first year of the "Benítez era", when from Holland he told me that Valencia had a lot of quality and that if things went just a little bit right and there weren't too many injuries, they would fight and win the League.

And the second, with me in Madrid on a very cold morning, next to the Abasota gym where he had once worked – and Rafa in Valencia, just back from a dreadful performance by the team, when he confessed to me: "Tonight I'm going on Canal 9 News and they're going to interview me. This is so you know that I'm going to tell them we're going to win the League. I'm convinced that we'll do it."

And he didn't get it wrong.

Two of my best friends: Paco, Paco Lloret, and Rafa, Rafa Benítez, brought together by this book written by one of them and starring the other. What more can I ask for? Both are benchmarks in their professions and share that exquisite taste for things done properly, in their personal and their professional lives.

Earlier I said that our friendship has brought about the friendships of our families as well. I would like to thank them both from the bottom of my heart for the way they acted towards my father, now passed away, and the blame they share for my blessed love of Valencia.

To you, Paco, for your affection, your support and your help during the hard times, which is when good people like you shine through.

To you, Rafa, for your friendship, for your advice… and for keeping your word about beating Barça at the Nou Camp in the cold winter of 2003, and making my father weep with joy on his deathbed, and my mother and my children, and me, of course. And for knowing you are my friend, that you were suffering with me, which was a solace in our time of anguish.

Almost visionary predictions, statements, people, friends, loyalty, values… I've spoken of all of these. They and much more are recounted in this book.

So as I said before: two of my best friends got together to make us happy with a wonderful story. I've enjoyed reading it. I hope you do too. And, please, don't forget this because it's true: the friends of my friends are friends of mine, isn't that right Paco? Rafa?

Emilio García Carrasco
January 2005

>> CHAPTER I **AN UNFORGETTABLE CALL**

A THIRST FOR KNOWLEDGE
EMILIO AND RAFA
THE TV PUNDIT
A TIME OF OPPORTUNITY

1   AN UNFORGETTABLE CALL

The telephone rang at the appointed time. The introduction was succinct.

"It's Rafa Benítez, the Extremadura coach. I gather Emilio has spoken to you about me. I'm interested in getting videos of the second division games you show on Saturdays."

A long-standing personal friend of mine, Emilio García Carrasco was, at the time, a sports journalist with Telemadrid. He had spoken to me about Benítez on more than one occasion – and with extreme passion. For him, Benítez was an unrecognised talent, lost in the basement of Spanish football – someone needing an opportunity to demonstrate his sound judgment.

Emilio had acted as a go-between, and had passed on my phone number. And so, one Saturday afternoon in the autumn of 1997, I was at home, waiting for that call. It was the first time I had spoken to Benítez, although I knew him from a distance through his involvement with the elite of the Spanish football world – as assistant manager at Real Madrid and manager at Valladolid. Despite the enthusiasm of our mutual friend, Benítez's career to date didn't really inspire optimism – a fleeting appearance alongside Vicente del Bosque on the Madrid bench, and a dismissal from Valladolid when they had faced imminent relegation into the second division.

That first personal contact with Rafael Benítez Maudes went the usual way of conversations between a journalist and a manager when they talk for the first time. We spoke about football matters in general – he asked me about Valencia, about Villarreal, about coaches and players. He also showed an interest in the sports programming on Valencian television, with which I was involved, and we agreed the terms for sending tapes of the matches he needed. He spoke with a naturalness and showed an enormous interest and appetite for acquiring the maximum amount of information possible. These characteristics perfectly fitted the profile of the coach described by our mutual friend, who championed him and had an almost blind faith in his abilities.

Though the conversation lasted only quarter of an hour or so, by the end a kind of trust had been established. With my parting words, I rather cheekily sprang a question on him – almost a premonition – that even now, several years later, makes me smile.

"Emilio has said you're the ideal manager to make Valencia League champions."

Benítez accepted my challenge – an ambitious dream – and his reply left a door open.

"I'd love to try it; it's a shame that Valencia isn't in better shape, it's a club with great possibilities, it has almost everything. It lacks calm, but I'd love to manage there one day."

At that time, in the initial weeks of the 1997-98 season, Valencia were going through their umpteenth upheaval – it was a turbulent period at every level. The manager, Jorge Valdano, had been dismissed three weeks into the League. Three games, three defeats. The straw that broke the camel's back for their president, Paco Roig, was an 'illegal' substitution in a match. In Spain there is a quota for the inclusion of non-European players in any game, and when Valencia had played Racing Santander at the El Sardinero stadium this had been breached.

Benítez was an unrecognised talent, lost in the basement of Spanish football.

When I had my first conversation with Benítez, the Mestalla club was immersed in a difficult transitional period. Claudio Ranieri had arrived and his approach to football was diametrically opposed to that of his predecessor. It was a period of radical change, a new system, and a different approach – even as far as dressing room cleanliness. The team couldn't settle and focus.

Gradually the 'stars' began to leave: Romario, Ariel Burrito Ortega, Marcelinho Carioca, Saib. Results failed to materialise and the Valencia fans demanded the dismissal of the chairman. Paco Roig left the club at the beginning of December 1997 with Valencia next to bottom in the League.

At that time, Benítez was working with Extremadura at Almendralejo – his sights set on getting promotion to the first division. The team had already spent one season in Spain's top division but had been unable to stay up. Now they were trying to get back – trusting in their coach, who would at the end of the season get them there. Villarreal, a club which had never been in the first division and which Benítez knew inside out thanks to the video tapes of their televised games, would also go up with them. A year later though, in the last game of the season, both teams were doomed to play each other for the right to stay up. In the end the result was a draw, which led to them both beginning a return journey to the second division.

He had to deal with both promotion and relegation.

And so, on Extremaduran soil, Benítez had his first major experience as a manager – a two-year period in which he had to deal with both promotion and relegation – an experience which would toughen him up and provide him with a wealth of knowledge for the future. A hard lesson, but a necessary complement to the many hours of analysis and study, and, above all, watching football at every level, from bottom of the table sides to the first division. And, of course, studying training methods in Spain and abroad.

A THIRST FOR KNOWLEDGE

Football is a vocation that has determined his life from an early age. Benítez lives for football, he is devoted to the cause. It is as if he were a researcher determined to discover the key – the secret formula which will unlock and decipher the mastery of this wonderful game. His thirst for knowledge knows no bounds, and his perfectionism devours hours and hours with no thought for the passage of time.

Before I knew him I imagined Benítez to be the typical swat, or perhaps that zany professor who locks himself away in his laboratory, losing all perspective on the world in his thirst to get to the bottom of everything. That is how our priceless friend Emilio had described him to me. The classic know-all who can fill the blackboard with arrows that show the tactical movements of Sacchi's famous Milan team, which astounded the football world at the end of the eighties and established its dominance for several years.

But of course, friends always tend to exaggerate virtues and play down defects. And so, I didn't really take Benítez's chances of becoming a successful coach too seriously. I have followed Valencia as a journalist for more than twenty years. It's a club I've loved since childhood. Now though, I have to confess that I never thought that Benítez would move on to manage Valencia, or Liverpool, nor, needless to say, that he would be capable of bringing so much glory to the two clubs.

EMILIO AND RAFA

My friendship with Emilio García Carrasco was forged during the Wimbledon tennis tournament of 1990.

Emilio had told me that he and his father were avid Valencia fans. A pleasant surprise. It was rare to find Valencia supporters from around Madrid. He told me his family background, and of the devotion of one of his grandfathers to the small town on the Turia, which he had often visited as a railwayman. In the harsh post-war years of shortages and hunger, the fertile lands of Valencia were the larder for many Spaniards. These weren't times of plenty, but at least the farming resources helped to alleviate the basic needs of the population. Oranges, vegetables and rice were essential staple foods in those terrible years.

At that time Valencia football club had a legendary team which dominated Spanish football taking three League championships and playing five Cup Finals. All in all, a team which attracted acclaim.

Emilio's father went to Valencia's matches every time they played in Madrid. He never missed going to the base camp hotel and remembered those days wistfully. And so, like so many others, Emilio became a Valencia supporter through a passion handed down through two generations. Emilio would go to matches with his father when he was a child, and had his photograph taken with his idols: Claramunt, Sol, Quino, Valdez, Keita and other members of that team at the beginning of the seventies.

An Unforgettable Call

THE TV PUNDIT

Emilio went into sports journalism and it was there that he met Rafa Benítez. Both were starting their respective careers when they met. On Telemadrid they formed a duo for all the televised second division games. It was the start of their friendship. It's not hard to imagine their long chats during car journeys on their way to matches, their shared lunches and the subsequent post-match analysis. Benítez is capable of talking about football for hours, he can't stop. In those days, the enthusiasm of someone making his way and yearning for the chance to show off his talent led him to convey his ideas to anyone who would listen, and who shared his way of thinking. Benítez found in Emilio García Carrasco such a person, the attentive listener. He imbued him with his football philosophy and convinced him of his promise. Emilio, who by then was already both my friend and a professional colleague, had no doubts.

At the time of our first meeting in London, in the summer of 1990, Valencia had been showing excellent form. The League had been a victory parade for Real Madrid – this was the height of the so-called "Buitre era". Real had beaten all the records, winning five League Championships in a row. All that remained beyond their grasp was the European Cup. An object of desire out of their reach. They couldn't even get to the final.

Valencia itself was making an impressive resurgence. From having been a second division team, with little more than 15,000 members on its books and a huge deficit, it had moved to being runner up in the League. Now it was back in Europe, doubling its membership and putting its finances on a sound footing. It just needed to climb one step further up the ladder, the most important step – to start winning titles again.

At that time Barcelona had already begun to forge the unforgettable "Dream Team" which would inherit Madrid's mantle and achieve the feat of four League titles in succession. To the traditional opposition from Madrid and, to a lesser extent from Atlético, would be added, halfway through the decade, the surprising emergence of Deportivo La Coruña.

And Valencia? They didn't climb that step, they came close to becoming Cup Winners but lost in the final. They also had a chance to win the championship on the last game of the 1995-96 season but, in the end, it went to Atlético Madrid.

Just as Benítez had said, and the majority of Spanish football fans had thought, Valencia never made the most of their potential. Despite having an impressive squad, talented players, good facilities, and many faithful fans, something always went wrong. They were a team which was comfortably in the top group, but unwilling to compete for titles with the traditional leading teams – content with a supporting role. Even when circumstances were in their favour, they still failed for one reason or another.

Benítez is capable of talking about football for hours, he can't stop.

Luis Aragonés' season was the exception. He instilled in the squad a non-conformist spirit and a way of operating which allowed him to get them within a stone's throw of glory. The rest of the managers, despite the reputations they brought with them, failed to achieve the expected leap in quality. Neither of the most illustrious pair, the Dutchman Guus Hiddink or, even less so, the Brazilian Carlos Alberto Parreira, achieved that aim.

For that reason, my friend Emilio, like so many others, despaired – sooner or later his Valencia always floundered – never quite managing success. Though the squad had players of proven quality, there was a complacency which he deplored. They always seemed to lack the necessary fight to win titles.

A TIME OF OPPORTUNITY

Emilio felt that Benítez should have an opportunity. I agreed with him, I sided with him – but really just to shut him up. I never seriously thought that a coach, as low-profile, and unknown to the public at large was going to be able to get Valencia to break that spell. I certainly didn't expect that with him they would, in three seasons, win the League twice and the UEFA Cup in their only double in 85 years of existence. If a World Champion with the Brazil national team or a European champion with the Dutch team PSV hadn't managed it, it seemed unlikely that a fairly inexperienced coach with a middling record would. However, before Benítez arrived on the banks of the River Turia, things had started to improve.

Ranieri took Valencia to the Spanish FA Cup after some memorable games in the qualifying rounds against Barça and Real Madrid, the sacred cows of Spanish football. And they qualified for the Champions League for the first time. Héctor Cúper further raised the bar, exceeding all expectations by getting Valencia through to two finals of the Champions League, the most important competition at club level. Two magnificent seasons – yet a bitter-sweet memory at the end of the day.

Then Benítez arrived. The situation at Valencia was better. The historic deficit that had dogged the club had been mitigated, at least in part. No doubt destiny, disguised as chance and necessity, brought him to a bench that was not intended for him. It left me perplexed because the wish of a friend had, with a little good luck, come true. Now he ventured to predict: "Valencia will win the League."

Many years later and with great satisfaction I've no choice but to agree that he was right.

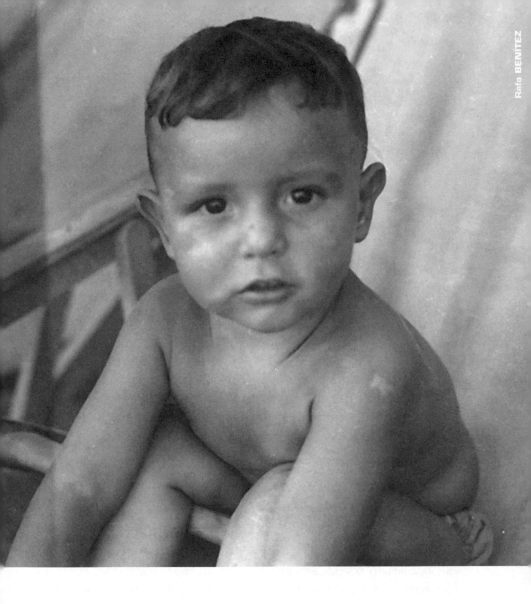

>> CHAPTER 2   **A CHILD OF THE SIXTIES**

A STUBBORN STREAK
CHESS MASTER
MEDICAL MAN
A VERY PRIVATE MAN

2   A CHILD OF THE SIXTIES

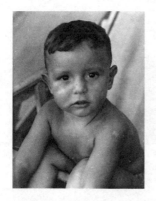

Rafael Benítez Maudes was born in Madrid on 16th April, 1960, into a middle class family. His father, Francisco, worked in the tourism industry and was a director of one of the most important hotels in the Spanish capital. He also managed a travel agency and a hotel group with hotels in several cities. His mother, Rosario, was a nurse, working at the La Paz Hospital and also in Móstoles.

Rafa is the second child of three. His brother, Francisco, was born a year before him, whilst his sister, Rosario, baptised with the same name as her mother, is several years younger. Both studied veterinary science, a profession which his sister currently practises.

The football environment in the Benítez-Maudes household broke the traditional mould. His mother was a great football fan, whilst his father followed it less fervently. They also supported different teams; his father following Atlético Madrid, whilst his mother was a faithful supporter of Real Madrid.

A STUBBORN STREAK

According to his mother, Rafa Benítez was mischievous as a little boy although he later became a studious, serious and responsible child. His father, Paco Benítez, confirms this, and with great pride paints a picture of his son's childhood – of a boy who never had any problems at school. He does however point to a streak of stubbornness.

"He sometimes insisted on taking a particular path. I tried to take him down another but it wasn't humanly possible to convince him. One day he fell over because he wouldn't listen to me. Although he hurt himself, he swallowed his tears and didn't cry."

Clearly a certain obstinacy was already evident in childhood. Rafa Benítez knew what he wanted and would do what he could to get it.

His early years were spent on General Romero Basart Street in the popular area of Madrid called Aluche. The Benítez family later moved to Majadahonda on the outskirts of the city where they stayed for a few years before finally settling in Pozuelo de Alarcón, a town near Madrid.

The relationship between Benítez and sport started at an early age. His father instilled in all three children a love of sport, from judo to swimming and, of course, football. At an early age Rafa could swim well. He also took part

His mother's influence led him to become a follower of Real Madrid.

in several judo competitions, a sport in which his brother was to achieve a black belt and win several championships. Over the years though, Benítez was to discover another passion – chess, a game in which tactics and strategy play a predominant role.

Benítez can remember the first football match he ever saw.

"I followed it on television since my parents didn't usually go to the matches."

In fact, he preferred to play football rather than to watch top flight games. The first side he professed any admiration for was the wonderful Brazilian team which won the Mexico World Cup in 1970. Captained by Pelé, this had a dream line-up of strikers – Jairzinho, Gerson Tostão and Rivelinho. At club level, his mother's influence led him to become a follower of Real Madrid.

Like so many other Spanish boys of the 1960s Rafa began playing football in the street. Here, he and his friends could contest their never-ending games, thanks to the absence of traffic, or they would play on the vacant plots which were later to be swallowed up in the boom of the construction industry.

Rafa Benítez also collected football cards and learnt by heart the names of the players in the football teams of his childhood. Also popular with children at that time were "bottle tops" on which were printed the faces of footballers and cyclists. Rafa spent many hours playing with these.

Another frequent venue for games was the school playground. It was here that he spent many hours, and where his skills began to become apparent. Benítez went to several schools, including Apostle Santiago School in the

Salamanca district, one of the most exclusive areas of Madrid where some of the most well-to-do families sent their children. As the family home was a long way away, he travelled each day by bus – always the first to be picked up and the last to be dropped off. This meant that he had to spend several hours on the bus, and eventually his parents decided to send him to another school, De La Salle, before he eventually moved to San Buenaventura on Portugal Avenue where he spent most of his school life.

His impeccable academic record shows that he was a keen pupil, organised in his schoolwork and willing not only to study what was required, but also to delve into subjects in greater depth He also took in what his teachers had to say, was never disruptive and was particularly keen on sports.

Rafa with his mother, his brother and his sister.

It was here that he achieved his first successes on the pitch, with the school football team, which also included Ricardo Gallego, later a Real Madrid player and an international.

The Benítez-Maudes family fitted the social profile of the new middle class, which was emerging in the larger Spanish cities in the 1960s. As the Spanish economy accelerated, the standard of living was improving and new habits and fashions were changing the country. At the age of seven Rafa took his first communion with his brother, dressed in a sailor suit as was the norm in those days.

'Falín', as he was called at home, always came back with good school reports. He was able to balance study and sport. He liked to make the most of his time and was methodical. And he made sure that he kept himself fit. Each morning he would get up early, run around the block several times, before

*Rafa and his brother Paco (Francisco) on the day of their first communion.
Both are wearing sailor-suits, as was usual in the 1960s.*

coming back home, taking a shower and then going off to school.

Like many others, the Benítez family would go to the Madrid hills for the summer, to Collado Villalba, a small traditional holiday resort town. Sport occupied much of his time, including football and swimming tournaments, which he would not only participate in but also organise.

The two brothers, Paco and Rafa, engaged in a bitter rivalry in the swimming pool. Despite his elder brother's superior technique and physique, Rafa's pride and determination enabled him to beat his brother on more than one occasion. His ability to lead was also evident at an early stage, when, aged just thirteen, he trained a children's football team in the mornings then in the afternoon worked as a gym instructor for the mothers. Benítez loved sport and coming into contact with people. He enjoyed teaching and helping those who had no special talent for sport. His patience and his teaching abilities endeared him to many people.

CHESS MASTER

Chess has been a lifetime passion for Rafa Benítez. It has also proved an enormous boon to him. Thanks to his love of the game, Radomir Antic took him on Real Madrid's trip to Italy in the summer of 1991 in preparation for their coming season. The Yugoslav coach, an accomplished player himself, was looking for someone to share his chess board with in his spare time. Despite being a member of one of Real Madrid's lower-ranking teams, Benítez was chosen and was therefore able to gain his first experience with a professional team.

Chess has been a lifetime passion for Rafa Benítez.

During his military service, too, chess offered him a safe passage. His skill at the game led to him being excused some duties. By then Benítez was already studying at the National Physical Education Institute (INEF) in Madrid. He had requested a deferment of National Service on the grounds of his studies until, on the third draw, he was given a posting in Madrid, which he took. The first two postings would have led to him being stationed on Tenerife, where years later he would not only achieve one of his first major successes as a manager, but also find the springboard he needed to move on to Valencia and consolidate his reputation.

The polytechnic military academy was in the area close to the Bernabéu stadium, and here he spent his military service in an easy-going way, with no pressure. His temporary enlistment in the army did not stop him from continuing his sporting activities – nor did it prove an obstacle to finishing his university studies.

MEDICAL MAN

Paco Benítez wanted his son to be a doctor. Rafa even got as far as enrolling at the Faculty of Medicine where he completed the first year, but he gave up medicine and concentrated on physical education – the demands of his footballing career preventing him from taking two degrees at the same time. However, that experience and the related studies, have given him a desire to deepen his medical knowledge and to apply it to football.

A story from a training session with Valencia FC illustrates this. One of the star players on the team was doing some muscle stretches after a hard training session. Benítez noticed that he wasn't doing them properly. He stood beside the player and entered into a very detailed explanation of how he should do them and the beneficial effects this correction would bring about. The footballer felt snubbed and, unaware of Benítez's earlier training, retorted: "Come off it, boss, you don't mean to tell me you know about medicine too!"

At INEF, Benítez opted to specialise in football. It was his vocation and also a way to get subject credits for the course through which he was to gain the national qualification of coach.

This was held in Albacete during the scorching summer of 1989. The candidates were brought together for a month and from that year group emerged, amongst others, some well known former players from the Spanish League, such as the goalkeepers Esnaola and García Remón and the talented inside forward, Julio Cardeñosa.

Benítez obtained his qualification without difficulty, surprising his fellow students both with his command of the theoretical aspects, and the ease with which he passed the practical.

"He coped as if he had played all his life in the first division," one of his colleagues recalls.

From his time at university Rafa retains an indelible memory of one of his teachers, Felipe Galloso, who had a considerable influence on him. A perseverant student, Rafa was never satisfied with doing the minimum, but always sought to broaden his knowledge – to go beyond what was strictly necessary. He rose early, at 6.30am, to catch the bus and then the underground, so that he could get to class early, and be able to train later. This desire to learn and a constant eagerness to better himself enabled him to maintain a close relationship with his teacher who could discern in Benítez great leadership and teaching qualities. Sadly, this relationship was unexpectedly and abruptly ended when Galloso was killed, in the mid 1980s, in a plane crash caused by fog and in which two aircraft were involved.

Rafa had been very fond of Galloso and held him in great esteem. It was a poignant moment, the worst of his time at university.

A few years later, with his appointment as sports director of the Abasota gym, one of the best known in Madrid, Benítez was able to put into practice his leadership and teaching skills. His work at the gym allowed him to organise specific training sessions and develop fitness routines, an enriching experience which he would later apply in his career as a coach. The gym attracted a range of people: members of the Spanish Royal Family, well-known Spanish singers such as Ana Belén and Miguel Ríos, important politicians and financiers as well as some famous sports people. When his activities as a coach started taking up more time he was obliged to delegate some duties and use his dinner hour to supervise work. That experience in the exclusive Madrid gym also had decisive repercussions on his private life. It was here that he met his future wife, Montse, a Doctor of Law, born in Orense.

From the weight training room to the altar steps. This was the route he took.

Rafa and Montse had been together for a number of years when, in the summer of 1998, they married in Madrid. Benítez had just taken Extremadura up to the first division, and now their honeymoon took them off to Italy – to Rome and Florence – though he was still able to sneak off and do some work. Some jokingly suggested that his obsession with football meant that his real objective in going to Italy was to visit Milanello, the famous sports centre of AC Milan, though that summer the focal point of football was France, where the World Cup was being held.

A VERY PRIVATE MAN

Rafa Benítez usually takes refuge in the privacy of his own home during those few moments when he disconnects from football. He has a strong desire to stay at home when professional commitments allow. He likes to share these rare moments with his family. It is an aspect of his life shielded from everyone else. Access is strictly limited. Rafa doesn't want football to encroach, and he keeps both worlds rigorously separate.

They are different realities and no exceptions are allowed.

Rafa and Montse have two daughters. Claudia, who was born in Madrid the year after their wedding, although at the time the family were living in Almendralejo, and Agatha who was born in Valencia in the autumn of 2002.

Jealous of his privacy, Benítez and his wife don't usually pursue an active social calendar, and their lives are spent more privately. Perhaps this desire for personal discretion provides him with the tranquillity he needs to achieve focus in his professional life. It is the essential foil. Montse keeps a prudent distance from football. She is not exactly a great fan and her public appearances are few and far between. During their time at Valencia she didn't go to matches regularly, though she did travel to Sweden to be at the final of the UEFA Cup in May 2004 and a few days later she was seen together with their daughters on the pitch at Valencia's Mestalla stadium during the pre-match ceremonies.

That was Benítez's last fixture at the helm of Valencia.

It was also the end of a monumental fiesta. The atmosphere on the terraces was electric. That night the club displayed to the fans both of the trophies it had won. An hour after the end of the game, thousands had gathered outside the stadium, hailing Benítez and clamouring for his appearance. Benítez, accompanied by his wife, appeared on the balcony to answer their appeal.

It was his last contact with the Valencia supporters.

Rafa BENÍTEZ

>> CHAPTER 3   **DREAMS OF FOOTBALL**

JOINING REAL MADRID
A CHANGE OF DIRECTION
STARTING TO COACH
FIRST STEPS
TIME TO MOVE ON
THE END OF THE LINE
IN THE LAND OF THE CONQUISTADORS
SUCCESS AT LAST
THE STRUGGLE TO SURVIVE

3   DREAMS OF FOOTBALL

In the end it was his father who decided to take the plunge.

"I have a twelve-year-old boy who plays football, I think he's a decent player, everybody who's seen him says so, I'd like you to give him a trial to see if he's any good."

These are words that must have been repeated so many times and will continue to be so. Boys with the ability long for a career in football. To assess their aptitude they must pass trials if they want to get into the top football teams – by their side, hopeful fathers who dream of seeing their sons become stars.

This happens daily in every corner of the world. It is how many football careers start, though the majority are dashed on the long and winding road in search of glory. Many are called but few are chosen.

And so, at the beginning of the seventies, Rafa Benítez's father talked to a friend of his, the son-in-law of Santiago Zubieta, who was part of Real Madrid's coaching team and looked after football at grass roots level.

Rafael Benítez had his chance and took it. His qualities convinced Zubieta, who approved Rafa after seeing him play two matches. Rafa joined the juniors and began his preparation alongside other hopefuls.

His profile as a footballer matches the personality he would later show on the bench. Above all, he was prepared for hard work and wanted to better himself. A midfield player, with a calling to manage, he was skilful with both feet, and had a good eye for the game. He didn't stand out but he had good qualities and a voracious appetite to learn – a very solid player, not brilliant, but one who always performed well and showed exemplary perseverance. Amongst his most marked defects was that he wasn't very good in the air and possessed poor dribbling skills, but he made up for these with his assurance in passing the ball. He wasn't an outstanding striker of the ball, somewhat average, but his movements were well coordinated – not particularly quick, but someone who knew how to get into good positions. That was Benítez the footballer. He had good judgment on the ball but lacked agility when attacking. His natural position was central midfield. Here he felt at home and made his team mates play. Above all, he was a player at the service of his team.

JOINING REAL MADRID

At the age of twelve Rafa Benítez joined Real Madrid, and took part in a tournament in which teams were given the names of players from the professional game.

Thrilled to bits, Rafa had confirmed his father's expectations.

His mother was even more pleased. Her son was joining her team. It was a licence to dream. From an early age she had lived in a football environment, as her brother had played for a while in the third division. Rosario Maudes had travelled far and wide with her mother to watch her brother play. Now she was going to repeat the tradition, but this time she would be following her son.

His father's professional commitments meant that it was his mother who would take Rafa to the training sessions and pick him up afterwards. During the week they trained on a ground next to the Bernabéu stadium. On Saturdays and Sundays there were the trips and the games. Many hours spent waiting and keeping him company – the age-old story of the sacrifice that fathers and mothers endure when their children want to be footballers.

Rafa's first experiences as a spectator also date from that period. The club provided him and his team mates with tickets to watch the matches up in the third tier of the stand at the Madrid ground. They had to arrive an hour and a half before the start of the match to get a place on the terraces, along with the public. They arrived well stocked with sandwiches and drinks.

He still remembers some of the legendary European matches that he watched from this bird's eye view: an epic recovery by Derby County; Borussia Mönchengladbach with their stars – Vogts, Bonhof, Stielike, Simonsen and Heynckes; the crushing German machine that was the Bayern Munich of Maier, Beckenbauer, Höennes and Müller; or, years later, the tight marking of Pérez García on Kevin Keegan when Keegan was with Hamburg S.V.

A gallery of images engraved on the memory of a youngster, who went to watch football yet thought like a manager – Benítez deciphered the play and analysed tactics, worked out the qualities of various players and drew his conclusions. He liked to suggest how things could be corrected or improved.

I have never liked telling people off, I simply tried to explain.

Even at the age of fourteen he had been drawing up reports and scoring players according to their performance. Such an early interest surprised his father. The lad did not make his assessments for fun; he explained his notes, highlighting the best players and revealing their weak points. He still has the notebook that his father gave him and in which he jotted down his scores. He started doing this at the summer tournaments during his adolescence but it was a practice he would continue in later years. A precociousness which, as he says, astonished some of his team mates.

"When I played football, some of my team mates said that I talked to them too much. I couldn't help it, if I saw a defect I tried to rectify it, I did it for the good of the team, I have never liked telling people off, I simply tried to explain."

A SPARTAN REGIME

His career in Madrid followed the natural line of development: from juniors to the youth team, then through to the amateur team which played in the third division. The next step would be to sign for Castilla, the second team. In the process he played in National Championships, and important tournaments and experienced his first clashes with good teams. He lived solely for football, taking great care of himself, watching his diet, diligently sleeping the right number of hours each night, following his coaches' instructions to the letter. He applied himself to his training regime. He didn't go out at night or to discos. His dedication was such that his team mates gave him the nickname, Trina, after a popular orange soft drink whose manufacturing process didn't allow any bubbles. This Spartan spirit stopped him from drinking any alcohol, even the occasional beer. And to ensure that he got the set number of hours of sleep each night, no matter how interesting the film he was watching on television was, he would miss the end of it. The next day he would ask his brother what had happened. For Rafa Benítez, all his energy was focused on football.

However, destiny was to deal him a nasty blow, the ruthless face of sport was to affect his career at a key moment.

A CHANGE OF DIRECTION

In the summer of 1979 his life took an unexpected turn. Real Madrid had won the League. Valencia had beaten Real Madrid in the Cup Final with two goals by Mario Kempes, 'The Matador'. A few days after the final Benítez left for Mexico where the World University Games, the Universiade, were being held. He was a member of the Spanish team managed by Horacio Leiva, who years later became chairman of the National Coaches Association.

Spain had made its debut with a comfortable 4-0 victory over Cuba, with Benítcz himself scoring a penalty. The next fixture was against Canada. The match ended in a goalless draw but for Benítez it was to have very cruel consequences – consequences that were to rewrite the script for him. The prelude to the drama was a disputed ball in the first half that he thought was his. A Canadian player came in with a hard tackle, Benítez's leg dug in and he twisted his knee. There was no malice intended, it was just bad luck. A serious injury in the most important joint. The internal lateral ligament of his right leg had partially severed.

There was no malice intended, it was just bad luck.

An incorrect diagnosis by the doctor led to complications and an even worse subsequent treatment hindered his recovery. The doctor was convinced that he was only suffering from a sprain, and Benítez played on in that wretched game wearing a knee bandage. Following the instructions of his doctor, Benítez spent two more weeks in the Mexican capital alongside his team mates, but he didn't get better and didn't play again.

On his return to Spain, a thorough medical examination by Dr Herrador, Head of Medical Services at Real Madrid, showed the true extent of the injury. In those days there was no magnetic resonance scanning for diagnosis and the first arthroscopy operations – a revolutionary system which has contributed to the excellent cure rate for cartilage and ligament injuries – were only just beginning to be carried out.

Nowadays, with the advances in sports medicine, this injury would not end a player's career. At the time though, Rafa Benítez was faced with a dilemma; an operation or physiotherapy. He decided against the operating theatre, preferring to entrust his recovery to a long process of physiotherapy which he faced with patience and optimism.

The injury had come at a very bad time. Real Oviedo had been following his development and had shown interest in signing him. It had also already been decided that Benítez would play the pre-season in Castilla.

But now it all went up in smoke. His career was cut short and he was forced to start all over again. For three weeks he was in plaster. Afterwards, he worked hard throughout his six months recuperation period, but his knee didn't completely recover. He slogged away in the gym every day, pushing himself to the limit to make up lost ground. But the pain wouldn't go away, he suffered with tendonitis and the lack of stability in the joint made him very unsteady when he played the ball. And there was the psychological impact.

After a year of inactivity he was sent on loan to Parla, a third division club close to Madrid, where he again played football. He even returned to the Spanish national university side, which was involved in a friendly tournament in the northern Spanish region of Asturias – but it was not the same as before. He performed well but with limitations. His chance had gone. Football wasn't going to let him reach the top as a player. He knew it and had to accept it.

The injury at the Universiade had shattered his dreams; despite all his tireless efforts and the sacrifices he had made, it prevented him from having the opportunity of playing at the top level, with the best players.

It also deprived him of what could have been a wonderful experience – playing in the Spanish FA Cup in 1980 in the Bernabéu between Real Madrid and Castilla. Castilla had had a spectacular competition knocking out several top sides to reach the final. In the final there were no surprises and Real

Rafa Benítez (bottom right) in a team photo with Parla.

Madrid became champions after mercilessly scoring against their second team – a team in which some players already stood out and would soon join the first team. Benítez, just turned 20, saw his dreams slip away. Words of encouragement and consolation from his family, friends and team mates didn't alleviate the deep disappointment he felt. All he could do was move on and set new goals for the future.

NEW AMBITIONS

His coach in the amateur team had already warned him.

"The majority of you will never get into the first division, your level is third division."

It was a cruel statement by Tomás Ramírez, but a true one. His pupils didn't want to believe it, but with a handful of exceptions, such as the wing back Chendo who made both the first team and the Spanish national team, it was the reality. It spurred them on to work incessantly on basic skills, so that they could use these skills easily in the uncertain future which awaited Benítez

Rafa Benítez during his time with Parla.

Rafa **BENÍTEZ**

and his team mates. Relentless football without a break, the long ball on uneven pitches, playing the ref's blind side, awkward crowds, excessively compliant refereeing, that was the environment within which they were going to move, that is where they had to survive and overcome their disenchantment.

For Benítez it was first stop Parla, next Linares. There his short career as a footballer came to an end in 1986 at the age of 26. Those were his only seasons as a pro. When it comes to assessing his career, despite the disappointment, he found it a good experience, with happy memories and some friendships.

He spent five seasons at Parla, and contributed to the club achieving a settled position in second division B. He also got to know Manuel García Quilón, who would later become his agent.

Initially Real Madrid had put him on loan to aid his recovery. Eventually the break with the Bernabéu club came and he was signed by Parla. He knew that he wouldn't make the leap back up to the top level, and so he took it without resentment. His leg was holding out, but there were few guarantees. Besides, this option allowed him to carry on studying at the University, and to live at home with his parents, brother and sister. It suited him, it was the best solution, the most practical one.

At Parla, there were players who had already seen it all, such as Macua, from Osasuna in the first division, and others who were going to make the leap up a level, such as the goalkeeper, Antonio, who would later sign for Valencia. He was also under several coaches during his five years.

His team mates saw the trainer instinct in Benítez straight away. His methodical monitoring of the season was already suggesting signs that he was to become a coach.

"He wrote everything down, injuries, cards, goals scored from set pieces, those who scored against us. Nothing got past him."

Despite his seriousness, he had integrated well into the squad of players. He was the only player with a knowledge of English and his team mates often used to call upon him as an interpreter during their trips to Majorca, when they crossed paths with an attractive foreign tourist. Mention of the club brings back memories of the good atmosphere in the changing room, as well as the friendship he maintains with some of his team mates from that time.

STARTING TO COACH

Once his time at Parla was over, he moved to Linares. This was thanks to Enrique Mateos, the coach of the Andalusian team, and a former player of the glorious Real Madrid side that Alfredo di Stefano captained. Benítez accepted the offer for a season, the last he would ever play.

Mateos knew him well and had followed his career since he had played in the lower ranking sides of Real Madrid. He had faith in his ability and went all out to sign him. He remembers a number of stories.

"Rafa, a lot of bossing but not much running," was Mateos's verdict.

One day Rafa Benítez came on to the pitch in the final ten minutes of a game against Ceuta at the Linarejos ground as a substitute for an injured team mate. He hardly had time to warm up. Despite this, he gave a strong performance which pleasantly surprised Mateos. He moved around the pitch, managing the team authoritatively.

"Rafa, if I'd known you were in such good form I'd have played you the whole match."

No sooner said than done. The next game was in the Arcángel stadium against Córdoba. It was almost 40 degrees centigrade, and the heat was suffocating. Benítez started the match but his performance was nothing like the previous one:

"Rafa, a lot of bossing but not much running," was Mateos's verdict.

When he had been manager at Lorca, another second division side, Mateos had also come across Benítez. At the time Mateos's situation had been delicate, his team was not doing well and he was on the verge of being dismissed. The match against Parla was an important one for him and Rafa Benítez, playing for the opponents, seemed determined to win the match on his own, such was his motivation. Fed up of seeing the massive amount of energy from the man he considered his friend, he blurted out from the bench:

"Come on, Rafa, that's enough, stop running around so much, do you want to get me kicked out?"

At Linares, the complicity between coach and player reached its height.

Benítez, with the consent of the coach, acted as an assistant; he managed the fitness element in training sessions and was in charge of organising the warm up sessions for his team mates. Mateos let him take over that duty, he was his right hand man and, as a graduate in physical education by that time, he was more than qualified. And so, in Andalusia, Benítez cut his coaching teeth – but besides football he also took the opportunity that year to improve his knowledge of other sports.

LEARNING THE LESSONS OF OTHER SPORTS

Rafa registered on a short course as a basketball coach, a sport which in the mid-eighties had become very popular across the country, especially since Spain had won the silver medal at the Los Angeles Olympic Games. Interest in football, on the other hand, had waned somewhat. The attraction of basketball could be attributed to several factors, and its coaches were very different to the typical football coach, both in their appearance and in how they discussed things.

He also took the opportunity that year to improve his knowledge of other sports.

Football was based on tried and tested values, and those involved stuck to traditional beliefs and approaches which were rarely challenged. Of course there were exceptions. Basketball, on the other hand, was seen as more innovative and it exuded a sense of freshness.

Benítez was attracted by it. It's approach to tactics was vibrant. There was an exhaustive process to learn the variants in defence and attack. These were then applied in games, with passwords given to them so they could simply be called out as options to be used at any given moment. Everything was rehearsed, the moves, the marking – there was a solution for any eventuality. The way that the coach and players communicated was also very interesting. Rafa reflected how it could all be applied to the world of football. Basketball was based on study and analysis. Two elements which he believed were paramount in sport and which almost no-one applied in the football world, and even less so in the third division.

While at Linares, Rafa Benítez could also enjoy one of his other great passions: chess.

If this town is known for any sport it is for its famous international tournament, considered unofficially as the world championship – the Wimbledon of chess. Its roll call of winners includes the best players. That season, 1985-86, he hoped to be able to follow the tournament, which some months before Benítez's signing for Linares, the Yugoslav Ljubomir Ljubojevic had won.

Around that time the rivalry between Anatoli Karpov and Gari Kasparov began to emerge. For a devotee of chess, this town in the province of Jaén represented a fantastic opportunity to break into expert circles. His stay at Linares was short but intense. He had already taken the decision to hang up his boots and steer his future career towards coaching. He wanted to return home.

At the same time that Benítez was retiring, Spanish football was witnessing the collapse of one of its most illustrious representatives: Valencia FC were relegated to the second division, victims of serious football, financial and organisational problems. This apprentice coach could not have suspected that years later he would write the most important page in the long history of a club which was then floundering.

FIRST STEPS

On his return home he joined Real Madrid as a coach of one of the lower-ranking teams. Fernando Mata, fitness coach and a friend of Benítez, was his middleman and had spoken up for the young trainer before the club authorities. At 26 years of age, and with the title of junior and regional coach, Benítez was to have his first experiences on the bench when he took charge of the Castilla B youth team. It was the 1986-87 season. He remained as coach of this team for two more seasons.

He then moved up to the Real Madrid B youth side. It was the first promotion in his early career. He had already shown good management qualities which had not gone unnoticed by Luis Molowny and Miguel Malbo, the duo responsible for coaching at the club, nor by the manager Vicente del Bosque. He was to remain with this team a couple of seasons more – a period which coincided with the pinnacle, and the beginning of the decline, of the famous "Buitre" era at Real – with its excellent group of players who had come up through the youth and reserve teams, and who were skippered by Emilio Butragueño. This generation would mark a high point for the Madrid club.

Halfway through the 1990-91 season Rafa Benítez took a step up to the under 19 team, which competed in the premier division, the highest youth category.

CRISIS AT MADRID

By now, a crisis in the first team had forced a takeover on the bench. Welshman, John Toshack, was provisionally replaced by Alfredo di Stefano with José Antonio Camacho, coach of the youth team, as his assistant. Ramón Martínez, sports manager at that time, offered the youth team job to Benítez. With this team he managed to win the League and two Cup Finals. During his last season he won the double, after beating Barça in the final on penalties. His eight-year apprenticeship was completed in the summer of 1993 when he took over the second team at Real Madrid, no longer known as Castilla but as Real Madrid B. They played in the second division and Benítez had already worked with them as an assistant to Mariano García Remón.

It was a period of feverish activity, with morning and afternoon training sessions from Monday to Saturday, undertaking specific work in groups or with the whole squad, and travelling at weekends to the matches – sometimes, depending on the destination, with both teams.

When he became head of the second team he was already coping with ease. His debut couldn't have been better; beating one of the strongest sides in the division – Hercúles from Alicante by 3-1 at the Bernabéu stadium. With this promotion a natural cycle was completed. He had acquired a good grounding, he had developed his working methods and had obtained the necessary experience without having been subjected to too much pressure. A host of footballers played under his management over this period, some of whom he had followed closely when they were in other weaker teams – names which would become renowned in the not too distant future, such as Raúl, Urzáiz, Guti, Contreras and many, many more. A week before Raúl's first division debut for Real Madrid, he had been under Benítez's wing at Palamós. There, the forward had missed a couple of easy chances which would have given them victory.

ON THE BENCH

There are always unforeseeable events in football and these were to provide him with a unique opportunity. The 1993-94 season would enable him to make contact for the first time with the top division in football. Not long after the second half of the championship had started, Real Madrid sacked its coach Benito Floro after losing unexpectedly at UE Lleida's ground, one of the division's relegation candidates.

Ramón Mendoza, the club chairman, entrusted the management of the team to Vicente del Bosque, who took Benítez on as his assistant. The team were in a bad way after having lost two League Championships, which they appeared to have sewn up until the last game of the season. All the pundits had expected them to win.

With Cruyff's spectacular Barça bursting onto the scene, Madrid were doomed to remain one place below the Catalonian team. The wind was blowing in favour of the famous dream team whilst Madrid tried tenaciously, but with little inspiration, to recover their lost prominence.

The first challenge for the coaching duo would be to get them back on track in the League, the second would be an uphill struggle in the qualifying round of the Cup Winners' Cup against Paris Saint-Germain. By the mid-nineties, the French had put together a formidable team whose elaborate football made the taste-buds of even the most sophisticated palates tingle.

However, Real Madrid were on the verge of pulling off a dramatic feat in the Parc des Princes and, after an impressive performance, were only one goal away from qualification. The team had clearly improved but they were still a long way from challenging for the title, which was to be fought out in a

The Castilla B team which was the first one that Rafa Benítez coached during the 1986-87 season.

thrilling game between Deportivo La Coruña and Barcelona.

They were also out of the Spanish FA Cup, having met a Tenerife team in top form. Feelings had run high, to the extent that there were three sending-offs in the return match played at home. And so, at the end of the season, the only targets left were to get into the UEFA Cup and prevent Barça from celebrating their fourth consecutive League title.

It was the penultimate fixture and Barcelona were to visit the Bernabéu. Only a victory was of any use to Barça and, despite a tense and lacklustre match, they managed it by a whisker. A frustrating outcome for Real Madrid. Things were to get worse a week later when Deportivo La Coruña let the championship slip through their fingers. Deportivo, despite a numerical advantage against Valencia, were unable to score or to make the most of a last minute penalty. They had needed a win but could only draw. There was no doubt Johan Cruyff and his Barcelona team were very lucky.

For his part, Benítez had lived through an invaluable experience. The situation was complicated, marked by pressure, constant demands from the stands, and a media that was always on their backs. It was nothing like the placid job of working with youth teams. He had become hardened to adversity. He learnt a lot alongside Del Bosque, who willingly listened to the suggestions of a well prepared assistant who had learnt his trade away from the limelight, unobtrusively – but one who had his eyes wide open, and was willing to learn.

There had been no time for planning in the way that he would have liked. Solutions were improvised on the job, but it was a challenge that didn't allow for half measures; a baptism of fire in charge of a famous squad – but one in which inconsistencies were beginning to show. As a consolation for this fateful season, Madrid challenged for the final of a tournament unofficially dubbed the Copa Iberia (Iberian Cup) against the Argentinian team Boca Juniors managed by Menotti. They won both legs.

Madrid, tired of losing League games in Tenerife, decided to sign up the architect of their torturers. Jorge Valdano came from the Canary Islands to join them as coach for the next season with a view to putting paid to Barcelona's supremacy.

And Benítez returned to the second team – and the second division.

It was to be his last year at Real Madrid, a season marked by a difficult coexistence with the first team coach. Valdano would suggest that Benítez put certain players in his line-up such as Sandro – a classy midfielder from the

Benítez demanded greater sacrifices of him.

Canary Islands but an inconsistent player in Benítez's mind – or Paco Sanz, a limited player in Rafa's estimation, but one who happened to be the son of the vice-chairman, Lorenzo Sanz. All of this would try his patience and the disagreements with Valdano became irresolvable.

At the heart of it lay substantial differences in their approach to football. Valdano saw in Sandro a footballer who needed to be free from tactical restrictions so that he could give rein to his undeniable creative qualities, whilst Benítez demanded greater sacrifices of him.

The harmonious relationship between the two coaches was now a thing of the past, even though the Argentine coach had, on occasion, spoken of the excellent work done by Benítez, whose reputation as a dedicated student and trainer, and one with an impeccable schooling, gave him a certain amount of prestige.

Another coach who was becoming famous in those days, José Antonio Camacho, had also gained access to notes drawn up by Rafa Benítez, and had valued the way they had been put together and the evident tactical concepts behind them. Benítez realised that the time had come to go it alone. The future lay in a change of scene. The time had come to leave what had been his football home.

TIME TO MOVE ON

Almost half his life had been linked to the Bernabéu club. Faced with what was unfolding around him he decided to cut his ties. Furthermore, Valdano was becoming successful at a Madrid that proclaimed themselves League Champions and had inflicted a humiliating 5-0 defeat on Barcelona. It was a scoreline which compensated the Madrid supporters for some of the open wounds they felt. It also allowed them to forget other resounding failures that they had suffered that season; their surprising failure in Europe against the modest Danish side, Odense, and their early quarter-final departure from the Cup against Valencia.

Against all predictions and without knowing it at the time, he was to make his debut in the first division. In the summer of 1995 Benítez signed for Real Valladolid, a team which had been relegated to the second division the season before. Fernando Redondo, the club coach, had two choices. The Basque, Chechu Rojo, was the other managerial candidate but in the end, the chairman, Marcos Fernández, opted for Benítez. Reports he had received supported his choice and the close relationship which Valladolid had with Real Madrid paved the way to an agreement. Ramón Martínez, another man who knew both clubs well, recommended the signing.

Rafa got down to work, he studied the squad, agreed which players should be released and which new signings should be made with a view to gaining promotion. Everything went to plan. That summer the team gathered together in Los Ángeles de San Rafael, a town in the mountains of Segovia, to put the final touches to their preparations.

A STRANGE PROMOTION

On a sweltering August afternoon, as Benítez and his players rested in their rooms for a refreshing, after-lunch siesta, there was a phone call which alerted them to a surprising piece of news. Valladolid would play in the first division the following season.

A momentous administrative cock-up by the Spanish football authorities was to blame. Celta Vigo and Sevilla had not settled their payments for the previous year and, consequently, the Professional League, in line with its regulations, had relegated them on administrative grounds. That decision gave rise to a huge scandal and, as was to be expected, an irate protest from the fans of both clubs. In the end, after several meetings and an extraordinary board meeting, a compromise solution was agreed – as an exceptional measure the first division would be enlarged to 22 teams. Valladolid and Albacete, who initially had been relegated, would be given a second chance and the offending clubs, Sevilla and Celta, would also escape relegation.

This solution put paid to a scandal which threatened to paralyse the start of the season and its smooth running.

Agitated by the impact of the news, Camilo Segoviano, the team representative, interrupted Rafa Benítez's peaceful sleep. He met with an unexpected response:

"Let's not get our hopes up, let's go ahead with our plans and we'll see how this story ends."

This was the terse reply of a manager who calmly stayed in bed and went back to sleep. In the end though, what had initially seemed a remote possibility became a reality. Despite the understandable scepticism of the manager, they had reached their Utopia. It was a fortuitous event, but one which forced the club to modify its strategy. They had been putting together a squad for the second division and now they would be competing in the first. Benítez had brought three players from Madrid's second team but they needed more tried and tested reinforcements. There wasn't much time, though some last minute signings could still be made.

Benítez's debut in the first division was on the 3rd September, 1995 – the opening day of the 1995-96 season. At its José Zorilla stadium, Valladolid were taking on a Barceolona team that was beginning to fall apart after those marvellous years under Cruyff. The previous season they had not won any titles, nor would they win any in the current campaign. And, before the season came to an end they would also witness the dismissal of their Dutch coach, after seven seasons on the bench.

A fearsome opponent with which to begin the season, as well as the most prestigious manager at the time. They would witness Rafa Benítez's initiation into the big time.

It wasn't a good start; after what had seemed a very even match Barcelona scored two goals in the last quarter of an hour. The defeat had been allowed for in Benítez's calculations and he accepted it quite calmly. Their first away game wasn't considered winnable either. Luis Aragonés' Valencia awaited him at Mestalla – the team that would end up second, almost beating the Atlético Madrid side that went on to win both the League and the Cup.

At the end of the season, though, these were their only wins.

Valladolid lost by the smallest margin and put up considerable resistance. After two matches the white and violet team hadn't scored a goal and were at the bottom of the table. A demanding start gave way to a modest improvement against some of the lower quality sides. Benítez and his men were able to breathe a sigh of relief with two wins, against Tenerife and Real Sociedad, improving their position in the table and placing them in milder climes. At the end of the season, though, these were their only wins. Halfway through and Valladolid were already set on an inevitable decline.

"The team played well, the supporters acknowledged it, most of the press too, but results dictate in football."

This sums up the hard-working style of Valladolid. They appeared to be beyond reproach. They were carefully prepared but they lacked the substance to compete at first division level. Far from adopting a battle-hardened style to ensure staying up, Valladolid oozed good taste in their passing of the ball, they never adopted a defensive approach and they were an open team. Despondency was soon rife. Danger was obviously lurking. Some internal problems arose with certain players including the Honduran, Guevara, in whom Benítez had little confidence. More tricky was the relationship with the Yugoslav, Asanovic, a footballer with a difficult temperament who had had confrontations with some of his team mates. On more than one occasion he stood up to Benítez, who again had little confidence in him. Their disagreements became particularly heated when in one match the Balkan player, having only been on the pitch a minute, gave away an unnecessary and suspicious penalty. The result was that Valladolid lost. That incident annoyed Benítez and relations between the two of them worsened from then on. Asanovic was a man who had been called on to make a difference. Instead he had become part of the problem, not part of the solution.

"Training was a real spectacle," said some well-informed observers.

Benítez remained faithful to his principles. "Training was a real spectacle," said some well-informed observers. He worked intensively, subjecting his players to regular video sessions of which he was very fond and which gave rise to some mocking comments from them. Quevedo, a stylish inside forward from Cádiz, and with a sense of humour typical of his hometown, welcomed the coach back after Christmas with a sarcastic remark. There had been a car accident in which Benítez had skidded on a sheet of ice near his family home. It caused considerable damage to the car but no major consequences for its driver.

"Boss, we're glad you're alright and that nothing happened to you, we were worried that the video recorder would miss you."

THE END OF THE LINE

Benítez's adventure at Valladolid was now nearing its conclusion. The season resumed in the New Year. Scarcely had the second half of the season started than he was sacked after a crushing 5-2 defeat by Valencia in a mid-week match.

That Wednesday, 24th January, 1996, the board of Valladolid sacked their manager. The end of the line for Benítez – though the Castillian team taken over by the Chilean, Cantatore, would, against all odds, escape relegation.

Benítez looked to the future – but the sacking hurt him. It took him a while to come to terms with the setback, partly because of his inexperience.

He understood the reasons for his dismissal but it affected his spirits. Fernando Redondo, the club coach, left with him, a club stalwart who had been one of his most loyal supporters. Now Benítez was keen for revenge – keen to try his luck again. His next stop would be Pamplona.

Benítez looked to the future – but the sacking hurt him.

His new team, Osasuna, were in a similar situation to the one that he had found at Valladolid when he took charge, except this time there would be no miraculous move to the first division. They were facing their third season in the second division. Behind them lay a lengthy period of almost fifteen consecutive years in the top division – and some splendid moments, including qualification for the UEFA Cup. Above all though, the team had a remarkable rapport with its fans, who had transformed their Sadar stadium into an almost unassailable fortress.

Osasuna trusted Benítez to take them back up to the first division. The coach, Zubillaga, a former player with Espanyol and Real Sociedad, backed a 36-year-old manager despite his recent wretched experience on the banks of the Pisuerga. He put forward a long-term work schedule to develop a coherent sports project. The squad was a mixture of youthful home-grown players and the odd exotic signing. It was a time when money was flowing between clubs in a happy-go-lucky manner, following the application of the Bosman Case ruling. New television contracts were generating boom years in football. An inflationary current had taken over the majority of the teams both in the first and second divisions. Signings were the order of the day. Players from the most far-flung countries were arriving in the Spanish League.

His stay in Pamplona would be even shorter than in Valladolid. He didn't even make it halfway through the first season. After seven matches he was sacked. Everything he'd planned was thrown to the wind in the face of poor results. Nothing new. Impatience claimed its usual victim. Osasuna were plunged into a constant dilemma, build a team and at the same time develop a reserve of young players, two extremes which are not necessarily incompatible but which divided their supporters. Osasuna were to have three more managers that season, until finally at the hands of Enrique Martín they miraculously escaped being relegated by winning their last five games.

For Benítez, it was a second experience and a second failure. The setback at Pamplona was even harder than the first, although this time he was better prepared and was less surprised by the disappointment. He faced the misfortune with stoicism. A positive consequence of his stay in Navarre was his contact with Paco Ayestarán, the fitness coach, who from then on would always accompany him, and in time would make the trip to England to be alongside Benítez at Anfield. There was a total rapport between them. Ayestarán had been a footballer in some lower level teams in the Basque Country, he had been in Real Sociedad's second team, and also had a coaching qualification and was a graduate in Physical Education. Twin spirits. They talked the same language. Even though Benítez was only briefly on the bench at the Sadar club a staunch friendship sprang up between them. Ayestarán was to be more than a mere fitness trainer, he was to be his right-hand man, the person who would advise and listen to Benítez. His alter ego, his necessary complement, his confidant and friend. Together they were to form an inseparable partnership.

The brief experience at Osasuna left a scar on Benítez's morale. A self-confident person and a believer in his own methods, his first two stints as a manager on his own had resulted in failure. He was now in a world far removed from the protective mantle of a club the size of Real Madrid. He hadn't even been able to complete a season. Another slip up could doom him to obscurity. In the world of football, labels are easily given but hard to lose. His reputation as a manager was under serious threat. Knowing this and with an understandable fear of a further setback, he got his third chance. This time he couldn't fail.

IN THE LAND OF THE CONQUISTADORS

Third time lucky.

For Rafa Benitéz, the saying came true, although when he arrived at Almendralejo he approached it with a certain amount of caution, and not before ensuring that he knew what his new club was like, he asked friends and acquaintances, he made in-depth enquiries. Following his first two experiences his reservations were more than justified. Whilst this was unlikely to be his last opportunity, it was one at which he could not fail.

Extremadura were based in the last Spanish region to have a team in the first division. In 1995 this had finally been achieved when Mérida were relegated at the end of the season, and their place taken by the club from Almendralejo. In the end they couldn't keep up with the best teams, partly because that season the number of clubs to be relegated was increased – five clubs from the first division were to go down, four directly and another on losing the promotion game – so that the division would reduce back to twenty teams.

When Benítez came on the scene, in the summer of 1997, he had one aim: to return the team to the first division. There were many changes in the squad as a result of the team having dropped a division but Benitéz kept the core: a group of players who had been linked with the club for some years. Some had played for the team in the third division and had lived through the rise of a club which, despite its limitations, had climbed to its peak. The chairman had spent most of his life in the job and the supporters welcomed Benítez's appointment with anticipation. There were no fervent demands, but they did dream of getting into the top division again.

In any team there is always a backbone of players who are firmly committed.

Down to work. In any team there is always a backbone of players who are firmly committed to their 'project', and this must always be taken into account.

Benítez and Ayestarán shared their second experience in a friendly town where they settled down with no problem. The coach was at ease, even though there were limitations when it came to training because of inadequate facilities. Benítez waited anxiously for the start of the season as though it were a final exam. He wanted to know if his view of the team would be confirmed when the moment of truth came. From what he had seen in the pre-season he had confidence in his players. Ahead lay a very demanding championship after the clearout from the first division, with several more glamorous contenders aiming for promotion. A long list of favourites, including Extremadura, was to be found in all the betting shops.

The season couldn't have started better. The team chalked up three wins in their first three games and by the fifth week they were top of the league. All the good omens had been fulfilled and Extremadura seemed to have the better of most of their opponents. It was to be a long season, forty-two matches, but the squad behaved reliably even during the bad times. The first loss didn't come until the seventh week of the season and happened at the ground of Atlético Madrid's second team. A setback that didn't spoil Benítez's plans. The team remained at the top end through constant hard work; they never gave the impression that they had missed the promotion boat.

This view was further confirmed in the second half of the season, the decisive stretch, when Extremadura opened up a gap between themselves and their pursuers and settled into second place, which would give them automatic promotion behind an impossibly good Alavés who would end up champions. The supporters at Almendralejo began to celebrate their promotion even before the season had finished. After an unexpected defeat at home against Toledo, a series of four consecutive wins put them on the threshold of the championship in the penultimate fixture. On the 9th May, 1998, they won away to Orense by the narrowest of margins. Almost five thousand supporters had gone with them, but the party began the next day when promotion was guaranteed after UD Las Palmas lost against all odds at the Insular stadium. At midday on the Sunday, news reached Almendralejo and its population of 25,000 inhabitants. There was euphoria. A spontaneous gathering filled the stands of the Francisco de la Hera stadium from the early afternoon. The squad and the coaching team turned out to share in their success with their fans. Benítez was carried around the pitch shoulder high.

SUCCESS AT LAST

It was 9th May, his first sporting success. That same day six years later he would win his second League with Valencia.

Pedro Nieto Cortés, chairman of Extremadura, had no doubts that Benítez should stay and consolidate the club's position in the first division. The rapport between them was good. Later there would be vehement disagreements, brought about by Benítez's insistence that suitable facilities be provided at the club. In the end he would get his way and a sports centre would be built, despite the chairman not seeing it as a priority. This was an issue that would divide them in the future, but at that joyful time the thrill of playing in the first division masked any problems.

They had achieved something that wasn't easy – they had regained their first division status a year after having lost it. With that achieved, and the dream of keeping the team up, Benítez faced the second season. Deep down he felt immense happiness at having broken the spell of his failed first period on the bench. Things had gone well, he was happy at the club and in the town. He felt supported though he knew he would be taking the field against the best clubs at a clear disadvantage. Some teams were light years ahead of them: Barça had come from conquering the double, the League and Cup; Real Madrid had won the Champions League against Juventus; Atlético Madrid had appointed Arrigo Sacchi; Valencia with Ranieri had grown in competitiveness, which would take them that year to be Cup Winner's in brilliant style; Athletic Bilbao were in the Champions League for the first time. His league was different, the Extremadura league was one of modest teams dreaming of being amongst the best – if they could take a swipe at them, so much the better.

He had the players convinced. It wasn't easy at the beginning. They had been used to a more informal relationship with Iosu Ortuondo, the coach who had taken them up the first time. A man who had done an excellent job at a club with no grandiose aspirations. Benítez's manner was more serious, with no close contact with the players.

The first unpleasant surprise for the squad was when he banned chewing gum. Initially they thought it was a joke, that he was pulling their legs. Nothing could have been further from the truth. It was deadly serious.

Benítez told the players that he didn't want to see anyone at training sessions or at matches with chewing gum. It didn't project a good image, and besides, it was dangerous, they might choke on it. They gave in. Another binding regulation had to do with their attire. Each of them dressed differently for training: some wore tracksuits, some cagoules, others shirts – a rainbow of colour. He told them that a halfway serious team had to be so even in the minutiae – even in things which might seem insignificant.

But what really astonished the squad was the training system.

But what really astonished the squad was the training system. They had never seen anything like it. Ayestarán made them work on their fitness until they were exhausted. They nicknamed him the Crock – "pain in the neck" – a term shared with the manager. Benítez repeated an exercise ad nauseam; they were fed up with his mirror theory. Benítez would pick up the ball – opposite him eleven of the players would be lined up as if they were playing a match. The coach would infiltrate their lines and the players had to move as if the opponent had the ball. In this way he put the pressure on, ensuring correct positioning as well as support from the other players. Without realising it, by repeating it again and again, the Extremadura players began to acquire responses which became instinctive and which, to their astonishment, began to appear quite naturally in matches. This invisible and apparently childish work produced a surprising result, which encouraged the players.

Work was planned down to the last detail. Many of the players discovered for the first time what a pulsometer was and what it was for. Their lactic acid levels were measured. They were at the forefront in training methods – at a club which, after four promotions in eight years, had gone from the third to the first division. The players got used to his methods, to his pre-match pep talks, they knew that he pushed them for their own good.

"From the tactical point of view he has been the best coach I've had. He prepared for the matches like nobody else," pointed out Félix Carballo, a veteran player from that Extremadura side, who personally experienced the full development of the blue and scarlet team.

At that time, before the games, Benítez would ask his footballers questions about their opponents, he stressed basic concepts, he didn't want any mistakes. He demanded that everyone pay attention and he even paired off the players in the hotel rooms where they were staying for the pre-game preparation according to their position on the field. His disciples, attentive observers who didn't miss anything, worked out that the initial line-up the next day would be based on this criterion. Benítez gave them no respite. At Extremadura they used the term "tormentor" for someone who allows no breathing space. Benítez was one in his pupils' eyes. At the same time they admired his wealth of knowledge and his industriousness. "He knew everything, you couldn't catch him out," the captain of the team at that time recalls, even though he personally had to face some monumental half-time team talks from Benítez.

THE STRUGGLE TO SURVIVE

It was no easy matter for Extremadura to stay up in the first division, but they nearly did. The start of their season wasn't good. Ironically, the fixture list meant that his debut with Extremadura was against Valladolid, his previous club. There were no goals that afternoon at Almendralejo. Two consecutive defeats against Barça and Atlético by the narrowest of margins put the team at the bottom of the table. The first sign of a response came when they drew against Betis, and with the seventh match came the first win against Alavés at Mendizorroza. Consecutive thrashings by 5-1 against Madrid and Celta Vigo saw a return to pessimism for the supporters, but immediately afterwards they celebrated their first two home wins against Valencia and Espanyol. A roller coaster of a ride!

The first half of the season ended with the team in the relegation zone. In the second half there was a marked improvement: Extremadura scored at grounds as difficult as San Mamés, Mestalla and Riazor, where they drew and were even on the verge of winning. They came closest at Deportivo where they scored an equaliser in the last minute, even though they only had ten men. At home they beat Betis, Atlético and Real Sociedad – the last match was talked about with suspicion, and with rumours of financial incentives, the infamous briefcases so much talked about in these situations. The Extremadura fans were still smarting over the draw with La Coruña the previous week when Villarreal arrived at the Francisco de la Hera stadium. Both teams were fighting for survival. The third team on the relegation list was Alavés who were playing at home against Real Sociedad. No-one doubted it would be a home team victory. Real Sociedad had nothing to lose and history suggests that the Basque teams usually help each other on these ocassions. This view seemed confirmed when the team from San Sebastián went ahead and the goal scorer, de Pedro, apologised. Alavés came back and won as was expected. For Extremadura, however, their future depended on their own performance. If they won, they were still safe from relegation.

The pressure was too much for Extremadura that afternoon. At half-time they were losing 0-2. Their second half response wasn't enough. They equalised against a rival side conscious of its status as unwelcome guest. Villarreal didn't have anything to gain from their performance. They were already in the relegation zone whatever happened. In the end the draw forced them both into the play-offs, before going down.

Despite the fact that Extremadura had achieved a not inconsiderable total of 44 points in the season – a figure which would usually have guaranteed them staying up – they had to go into a two leg play-off. Rayo were their opponents and everything went wrong for Benítez's team. In the first minute of the away game, they gave away a penalty and their goalkeeper was sent off.

It was the beginning of the end of a beautiful adventure.

Rafa BENÍTEZ

>> CHAPTER 4   **RETURN TO COACHING**

4   RETURN TO COACHING

After a year off, Rafa Benítez returned to coaching again.

The relationship with his agent, Miguel Ángel Cermeño, was ended and Manuel García Quilón began to represent him. They had known each other for some time. Both are men with strong personalities, who speak their minds from the outset. Ground rules were established, there was no signed contract but instead an agreement based on mutual trust. Quilón made it clear how he operated: at the slightest disagreement between them the arrangement would be cancelled and they would go their separate ways. This approach is not the only unusual thing about Quilón, a man who has excellent intuition in matters of football, and sound judgement when choosing footballers.

Both also share an ethos. They don't believe in the cult of celebrity and neither is dazzled by the glamour of the world of football. García Quilón knew that Benítez was a manager with enormous potential but he had concerns about his obstinate character and his pride. On his part, Benítez didn't want interference from anyone with regard to coaching matters and although he will usually sound out other views he doesn't allow anyone to meddle in his decisions – that is his terrain, his exclusive area of authority.

THE MOVE TO TENERIFE

The first opportunity to show his abilities took Benítez to Tenerife. It was the summer of 2000. The Canary Island club were in the second division. Memories of the team's success under the management of the German, Heynckes, were fresh in people's minds. Then, less than three years before, the club had found itself in the semi-finals of the UEFA Cup beating a number of major sides in the process. The eventual champions, the German team Schalke '04, had finally stopped them.

Tenerife fans had also lived through five years of unexpected prominence following the appearance on the scene of Jorge Valdano and Ángel Cappa in the summer of 1992. The Argentine duo had saved the team, which had not only seemed doomed to relegation but also faced a frightening fixture list.

Match after match the island squad won at home against the giants of the League: Valencia, Barça and Real Madrid. Their last game against Madrid was an epic battle and the result significant. Tenerife, already out of the relegation zone by then, had nothing to lose. They turned in a staggering performance. From a position of being two goals behind they managed a draw and in the process stopped Real Madrid winning the League.

The story was repeated the following season, Madrid were again to fail to win the championship at the Heliodoro Rodríguez stadium. It was another heart-stopping end of season match. This time though the Canary Islanders would, for the first time ever, go on to play in a European competition. Johan Cruyff's Barça were to be the main beneficiary; in both cases taking the Championship.

Now though, the glory days couldn't be revived. Much to the fans' desperation Tenerife had been in the second division for two seasons. Their chairman, Javier Pérez, was determined to pull the team out of the hole they were in and bring glory back to the club. Facing an extremely tough season, probably one of the most demanding in the club's history, he played the Benítez card.

Four teams stood out that year: Atlético Madrid, Sevilla, Betis and Tenerife. There were clashes in the second division that were much better than some in the first division. As the season wore on, the superiority of this quartet of favourites was confirmed as they fought tooth and nail to the end.

A SPLIT SQUAD

At Tenerife, Benítez faced a squad split into two clearly defined groups. On one side were the veterans, survivors from the club's glorious recent past, though also participants in its more recent decline. On the other, was a clutch of youngsters – not well known, but all aiming to conquer the world. They had come from various places, and some had trained in top teams. From this mixture of up-and-coming players would emerge the backbone of the team that he would take back up to the first division at the end of the season. Benítez put all his confidence in this group: Mista who had left Real Madrid in a manner which would end in the courts, Curro Torres schooled in Valencia but ignored by the Mestalla side after playing for Recreativo Huelva, Luis García from the Barcelona stable, Martí who had hardly played for Majorca, and the Mexican Torrado.

The environment at the Canary Island club was a very demanding one. Nobody on the island had accepted that the days of wine and roses were over. Here was a public that would not accept even the slightest failing. The pressure was stifling. Rafa Benítez had to remedy the situation and an even more dangerous one – the obvious dissatisfaction of one sector of the squad. The veterans had been demoted and were not happy.

Merits earned in the past are no guarantee of a first-team place.

One constant of Benítez's work ethos is that he doesn't like players who believe they have the right to play because of their reputation and experience. To him, merits earned in the past are no guarantee of a first-team place. Accustomed to enjoying preferential treatment, the footballers who had been with the club all their career found that they were not being given prominence.

The fans hadn't forgiven them for being relegated in the 1988-89 season. The team had had players of recognised prestige – players such as Makaay, Kodro, Emerson, Jokanovic, Felipe and Juanele – and so it just hadn't been expected.

As often happens when things start to go wrong, there was a lot of criticism, as well as rumours and all kind of remarks about the players' private lives – some well founded, others exaggerated – and the atmosphere at Tenerife was strained. These are the consequences of failure on the pitch.

The ambitions of the club were high. There was no target other than promotion. A year earlier Benítez had had the opportunity of going to Santa Cruz, but he'd preferred to wait. He didn't like the idea of taking over halfway through the season with lots of ingrained defects and little room for manoeuvre. He'd rejected Tenerife's offer but had agreed to start there at the beginning of the following season. When he arrived on the island he soon understood the position. Here was a club that had come down in the world and was now being forced to rise from the ashes. Still rooted in the past, it could not accept what it had to face up to – and even simple things such as equipment for training sessions were lacking.

Faced with this mindset, Benítez reacted with surprising temperance. This astonished many who had expected to hear his complaints, but he played down the situation, making light of the matter and trying to convince the players that the problems were minor.

Another conflict, one of internal structure, was added to the daily issues – the position of captain. Pier, who had held this post, was suing his old team Sporting Gijón for breach of contract and it wasn't known if he could continue in the team. The Argentine Lusenhof, on the other hand, resigned from the post because of disagreements with a group of the fans. In the end, at the express wishes of Benítez, the responsibility was given to Martí, one of the youngest players.

The start of the season was hopeful despite losing against Albacete in the first match. The team gradually improved, putting together three consecutive draws. In the eighth week they had their first thrashing when they lost to Betis. This acted as a spur for Tenerife, who then went on to win the next six games, including a very important one against Atlético Madrid, the main favourite, in a comeback at the Calderón stadium. It was the eleventh match and the Canary Island team moved to the number one spot. They would stay there for eight consecutive weeks until Sevilla, the other Seville team, beat them at home. There were twenty-three weeks to the end of the league season and though Tenerife would not take the lead again they would remain in either second or third, guaranteeing their promotion to the first division.

Throughout the season there had been difficult moments. A tough confrontation with the chairman, Javier Pérez, had led to a cooling of relations until they became non-existent. Benítez won't accept interference from anyone, including his chairman. And as all this proceeded he also had serious differences with some of the press.

Benítez recalled the advice of Fernando Castro, a coach who had preceded him on the bench at the club.

"I would always go out for lunch with the reporters who treated me the worst, to see if in this way they would change their views, but in the end I made enemies of those who treated me well, because they said I never had lunch with them, yet did with those who criticised me most."

Benítez opted to keep his distance from both his most bitter critics and his supporters. He didn't lunch with either group and so nobody could reproach him. And through his tenacity he began to gain the respect of the majority of the players and staff.

NEW OPPORTUNITIES

Halfway through the season he received an offer to return to Valladolid the next season. Santiago Llorente, sports director at Tenerife, his staunchest supporter and the man who had offered him the Tenerife contract, had left the club halfway through the season and gone to Valladolid. One of his first decisions was to offer Benítez a contract for the following season. Everything seemed to be tied up until Valencia appeared on the scene. Given the choice the coach didn't hesitate in his decision – Mestalla.

Santiago Llorente had to accept his decision, knowing that it was an excellent opportunity which Benítez couldn't turn down. With rumours of his departure for Valencia now circulating, Benítez achieved his target of taking Tenerife into the first division, thanks to the narrowest of wins in the last match at the Leganés ground.

His time on the island came to the best possible end. He had achieved the success he had wanted, as well as the respect of the fans.

A QUIRK OF FATE

Benítez sits in front of the television at home in Tenerife.

The Champions League final is being played in Milan. In the legendary San Siro stadium two teams traumatised by the competition are facing each other. Both have lost their previous two finals. Valencia and Bayern Munich come face to face. The Germans can't forget their bitter 1999 defeat by Manchester

Rafa Benítez celebrates the return of Tenerife to the first division.

United at the Nou Camp when the match they thought they had won slipped away from them in added time.

Valencia prefer to forget their final in Paris in 2000. Given that they didn't really seem to be there for that duel against Real Madrid, it's not surprising that they don't remember – a match decided with an emphatic 3-0 scoreline. Now fate has given both teams a second chance.

As for Rafa Benítez and his close circle, they had no idea that against all the odds, they would, the following season, be in charge of a team which could be European Champions.

Manuel García Quilón, his agent, was in Milan to watch the final and to be with the family of Rubén Baraja, a player whom he also represented. He met the Valencia directors and attended the dinner organised afterwards for the guests.

At no time was Benítez mentioned as a possibility, but for some time his name had been on the mind of Javier Subirats, sports manager at the club. The match itself turned out to be a disappointing spectacle, with both teams more concerned about not losing than about winning. Much the same as often happens in finals in this tournament. Inevitably the football is diluted.

It was a noisy event, enlivened by the Dutch referee awarding three penalties, two in favour of the Bavarians. The second penalty was not only very dubious but also enabled Bayern to equalise. Extra time. More suffering, even less football. No-one wanted to lose; nobody took any risks – although Zahovic threw away two chances which would have made him a god in the eyes of the Valencia fans.

All this was followed by that anthology of fear: the penalty shoot-out. Two giants between the posts: Cañizares and Kahn took turns to save each and every penalty. The suspense was prolonged. Another series of penalties. Valencia seemed close to victory but then Carboni's shot hit the crossbar. The second series was over quickly. Bayern took the title. For the second consecutive year, the Valencia supporters returned home demoralised and bathed in tears.

It was in that mood of bitter disappointment that the season came to an end, and with it the reign of Héctor Cúper.

Benítez had watched the match attentively at home; he had scrutinised it with his customary coolness; he had taken some notes; noticed some players; but he wasn't aware that the way events were to later unfold would affect him directly.

May came to an end. While Rafa Benítez fought bravely to put Tenerife into the first division, Valencia became immersed in the deepest of depressions as they failed to qualify for the next Champions League. They had lost the final and had failed to qualify through their home championship, unable to attain the single point they needed in the last two weeks of the season.

A defeat at Mestalla against Deportivo was the prelude to the disaster that was looming for them at Nou Camp. There they lost their ticket to the Champions League when, in the last moments of the last game of the season, with the score at 2-2, Rivaldo, who had already scored both Barça goals, added a spectacular third with his famous overhead kick. An acrobatic goal that put Barça through instead of Valencia.

By then, Benítez already knew that he would be manager at Valencia, though it had been a surprise.

Now it was well into the night at Barajas airport. Benítez had just taken Tenerife up to the first division. Two of his players were close by, Mista and Curro Torres. They were listening to the radio, following the events of the game with visible emotion. Both were also to join Valencia and had dreamt of playing in the Champions League. Though all three were to make the same journey, the manager kept his distance from his players. While they didn't hide their interest in the Barcelona-Valencia encounter and kept their colleagues up to date with developments in the game, the manager remained isolated from the situation that awaited him, taking hardly any interest in the final result. He showed not the slightest concern about what was happening, faithful to one of his principles, "If it doesn't depend on us or on our work, then we can't do anything about it."

He resigned himself to the vagaries of a destiny which was beyond his control.

An injection of optimism seemed a basic requirement.

That was the inheritance awaiting Benítez. A team that was in the UEFA Cup, but with its spirits shattered after both finals had been lost. The excellent European record of the Mestalla team had not been crowned, and glory had melted away in the decisive match. It was time to get back their self-belief.

An injection of optimism seemed a basic requirement. Benítez would apply himself to that task from the very first day that he arrived in the city – a city disenchanted and dejected after having lived passionately through Valencia's pilgrimages to Paris and Milan in pursuit of an elusive title. All that was in the past.

THE JOB NO-ONE SEEMED TO WANT

His arrival at Valencia was the result of a string of coincidences. Once the departure of Héctor Cúper had been decided, after the differences of opinion with a broad sector of the Valencia fans had become worse after their defeat in the Giuseppe Meazza stadium, the club set about looking for a replacement for the Argentinian manager.

Under consideration was a list of candidates, on which two reputable and prestigious Spanish managers predominated: Mané, the manager of Alavés who, against all odds, had taken his team to the final of the UEFA Cup, losing after a frantic contest with Liverpool in Dortmund; and Javier Irureta who, a year earlier, had conquered the League with Deportivo. Irureta was offered a very attractive financial deal by Valencia and was on the verge of accepting it.

After his success in the League with the Riazor team he had weighed up the risks of prolonging his stay at La Coruña and had readily considered the option of going to Valencia. The change of scene was attractive. Especially for him, a manager who had been based in the north since his beginnings with Sestao Sport Club. Almost all the most important teams on the Cantabrian coast had passed through his hands; Athletic Bilbao, Real Sociedad, Celta Vigo, Logroñés, Racing Santander, Real Oviedo, all in the first division and some competing in Europe.

It was the second time that Valencia had considered signing Irureta. The first had been a decade earlier, in the early 1990s, when the late Pasieguito included him on the short list of candidates to replace Víctor Espárrago. Irureta had been enjoying success at that time at Oviedo and took the players from Carlos Tartiere into UEFA.

The Dutchman Guus Hiddink was eventually chosen. Now, Irureta was again amongst those at the top of the list, though he wasn't initially the most favoured. Whilst circumstances would improve his chances and he would become firm favourite, in the end he decided against it and renewed his contract with Deportivo. The waters of the Mediterranean hadn't exerted their expected charm nor had the attractive signing-on fee that was being offered – even though it was considerably more than he had been offered by Deportivo.

Irureta took his time weighing up the pros and cons, he consulted with people from his inner circle and reflected calmly before making a statement.

His decision took into account that, at the time, Valencia were seen as being a difficult club. The climate of permanent conflict contrasted with the calm that Coruña enjoyed where the decisive leadership of Lendoiro, the club chairman, avoided any bad blood. Irureta didn't approve of the harassment that Cúper had suffered, relentlessly criticised by the fans despite having taken the team to two Champions League finals. Another weighty argument to be factored in was the foreseeable break-up of a squad that had already, that hectic summer, lost their talisman – Gaizka Mendieta.

Irureta's chances had increased when the original favourite, Mané, had backed out, reneging on a verbal agreement to manage Valencia. It had all seemed wrapped up when, suddenly, he changed his mind to the astonishment of some club directors whose interest in retaining his services was evident.

His refusal was based on similar arguments to those of Irureta. Valencia were going through a period of instability, the main shareholder was not a member of the board of directors, cock-ups were occurring on a daily basis – not the best working environment for a manager used to the peace of an organisation without that degree of outside pressure.

Mané didn't think about it as long as Irureta. He didn't fancy being swallowed up by a volcano in constant eruption. Even in the negotiation process there was the difficulty that he had to deal with several officials who assumed the function of directors of the club. This internal struggle was an added problem. Both Mané and Irureta concurred. They also sensed that the ambitions of the club were too high and felt that if Cúper had sustained insults, despite his two seasons, it would be more than likely that the heir would be subjected to a very tough examination. Mané predicted that these would be arduous working conditions, with little to be gained and much to be lost.

Valencia had not expected to have two rejections.

Valencia had not expected to have two rejections. Now they tried desperately to get Luis Aragonés to return – he had had an excellent season for them in the mid-nineties. That season Luis had managed Majorca, who had achieved a brilliant third place, the best in their entire history, and who would play in the next Champions League. The directors put an extraordinary offer on the table for him.

But the "Wise Man of Hortaleza" had already decided not to continue at Palma and had committed to Atlético Madrid. Now Valencia knocked on his door and offered him more money than the Calderón club. Luis listened – but he rejected them too. He didn't like it that they had come to him only after having been turned down by other managers. He also felt obliged to honour his agreement with Atlético, his lifelong club, where he had been a player and at which he had spent most of his time as a manager.

When Luis turned Valencia down he didn't know what division Atlético would be in the following season. At the time they were fighting tooth and

Valencia had now been rejected by three candidates.

nail to get into the first division. Despite the uncertainty, he stood firm and although there was no signed contract between them he honoured the verbal agreement existing with the Gil family, which governed the club. He would manage Atlético in the 2001-02 season. In the end he would do so in the second division, but he would achieve the objective of taking them back into the top division. He didn't back out, not even in June 2001 when Valencia made a desperate bid after Atlético had missed the promotion boat after a final best described as *not for the faint-hearted*. In the end, the two teams from Seville and Benítez's Tenerife were the ones to go up to the first division.

Valencia had now been rejected by three candidates and the situation was becoming worrying. A club that had twice been in the final of the Champions League couldn't find a manager. Initially, foreign managers had been ruled out – a policy the club had stuck to over the previous decade apart from the appointment of the Argentine, Carlos Bianchi, who had been successful with Boca Juniors, but not with Valencia.

THE CHANCE COMES

Then, Javier Subirats proposed an unexpected name to the Board: Rafael Benítez. Most of those present knew nothing about him. They knew nothing of his career. Not who he was, where he had come from, or who he had managed.

The looks of incredulity had been expected as well as the question "Who is he?"

Subirats patiently explained the salient facts, making a strong case for Benítez. In short, he took a gamble. He had the backing of Manuel Llorente, general manager of the club, who didn't enjoy the game of putting forward candidates to tempt the directors. Pedro Cortés, the chairman, also gave his blessing.

The unanimity amongst those who carried most weight in the running of Valencia tipped the balance. The proposal won, though guarantees were sought and Subirats had to sign a paper declaring that he would accept responsibility for the signing. Other board members accepted the decision reluctantly, some were openly sceptical and others took advantage of the situation to voice their comments.

The directors who represented the interests of Paco Roig, the largest shareholder, quickly showed their support. They joined the fray as soon as they could and took advantage of the available microphones to sum up their populist appraisal of the situation. The remarks of Marcelo Safont must rank amongst some of the most inane comments ever made. He attempted sarcasm and humour and achieved neither. In his attempt to deride the future manager he cracked a joke based around the surname. The legendary 1960s matador, Manuel Benítez, el Cordobés, had invented a famous bullfighting move known as the leapfrog, not one that he expected their new manager to be able to do. The supposed joke back-fired.

And so, Benítez came to Valencia – ready to win the most sought-after trophies at a fearsome club that more experienced managers, and ones of proven prestige, didn't want to take on.

Talks didn't take long. Subirats had already spoken to Benítez's agent after initiating secret talks. When he had offered the chairman Benítez's candidature he had already met with a receptive response. Pedro Cortés spoke that afternoon by phone with Benítez.

"Have you got the guts to manage Valencia?" he blurted out.

"Of course, I have. I'm not scared. You also have to have courage to manage at Tenerife," was the calm reply to the gauntlet thrown down.

Subirats was his true champion; he had taken the necessary steps off his own bat and presented the matter ready-wrapped to those in charge at the club. Subirats had been following Benítez's career for some time. He knew him well and had made enquiries with people close to the coach. The quality of play at Tenerife and the character shown by the team during several games that season had come to his attention. Their results and their position in the table confirmed his conclusion. He could sense that this was a coach to be reckoned with. They had both encountered each other in youth tournaments years earlier, and from then on he had followed Rafa's progress. His teams were well-crafted and gave off that unmistakable air of being well organised. He hadn't had a moment's hesitation when he suggested his name. Subirats was opting for radical change, for a young manager with quality, with the need to make a name for himself, eager to manage a big club and with a thirst for glory. He would demolish the more conservative arguments that pointed to established figures – managers with more miles on the clock but less ambition.

In his justification to the board he reiterated the resounding failures of the more well known managers who had sat on the benches of Mestalla in times gone by. Some had been flamboyant but had contributed nothing. Subirats himself had been a player with Valencia for ten years and knew the idiosyncrasies of the club perfectly – its needs, its defects. In this calm analysis, the figure of Benítez was not a media gamble but fitted in neatly with the ethos of creating the best possible Valencia, something Subirats had spent years planning.

A STRANGE COINCIDENCE

The chairman of Valencia knew very well who Benítez was. For years he had been friendly with Rafa's father as a result of his regular business trips to Madrid. Pedro Cortés used to stay in a hotel run by Paco Benítez. A coincidence, which was yet another piece of luck in this bizarre story. He remembered Rafa's father's flattering words, the recommendation for a son who was carving out his future: "Take my son to Valencia. He's a wizard, he'll be a great manager."

This time it was serious. The whimsical circumstances of fate were to bring his son to the forefront of Spanish football. It was his big chance. Benítez took the news with joy but with the moderation which he has always shown and which he has insisted his players adopt: "You must always keep up appearances and not lose your composure, not even in moments of the greatest euphoria," he said to the Tenerife players when they were organising an impromptu party after clinching promotion to the first division.

His teams were well-crafted and gave off that unmistakable air of being well organised.

The thrill of this success didn't cloud his vision, he still had his feet on the ground. Now he had a new challenge. Valencia offered him a two season contract, though his agent had tried to get just one. The strategy of García Quilón, who had blind faith in the coach, was quite clear. He believed that Benítez would triumph in a big way and that he could increase his value on the market. His name would begin to be on everyone's lips and he would be able to renegotiate his future in a year's time. A clear but risky strategy.

Nevertheless, in the end the club's proposal prevailed and Rafael Benítez's contract was agreed for the next two seasons. It was made public after the last day of the season. Benítez went up with Tenerife while Valencia remained in extremis, out of the Champions League.

A week later, Rafa Benítez and his wife arrived in Valencia on a stiflingly hot day. A mass of people turned up at the reception they later attended to welcome them to the club. Most were curious. Many were sceptical.

>> CHAPTER 5

LAW OF THE
DRESSING ROOM

5   LAW OF THE DRESSING ROOM

The dressing room has its own laws. There, in privacy, isolated from their surroundings, the players establish their own code of coexistence. This reality is accepted by every member of a club – including the coach. It is the sacred forum where the squad settles matters that affect it. Over a season all sorts of internal mishaps, problems and confrontations occur that need to be dealt with and sorted out. Generally, neither the coach nor the management take part directly in these types of conflict. They get news of them but they don't usually intervene. They respect the footballers' autonomy.

Every dressing room is different, but deep down there is a similarity. There are nuances, minor variations, but players develop similar rules of conduct. It is a 'family' coexistence in which members have a shared loyalty, leaders appear who call the shots, there can be antagonism between members of the clan, tense moments which cause friction and in which each faction views the situation from differing points of view.

This is the daily reality of a changing room over a season. If the results are good then everything is easier, but if not, control of the situation and the ability to respond will be tested. This is something of which the manager is aware, and it is a background against which he must carry out his job. He must keep a balance and not come down in favour of some players at the expense of others. The first target for a new manager is to win the confidence, and especially the belief of his players. There will almost never be unanimity, but a manager arriving at a club knows that his first target is this: the squad must respect their manager and believe in him.

When Benítez arrived at Valencia there were doubts as to whether he would be able to exert authority over a squad that had far more experience than he had in top flight football. This didn't worry Rafa Benítez. Confident of his abilities and, above all, in his conviction, he was not afraid of the challenge. From the very first day he applied himself to the job, conveying a message of hard work and improvement. The dressing room quickly caught on. It was a process of natural assimilation, with no traumas. The team accepted his methods and knew that the man in charge, the person who would lead them, was totally competent even if he wasn't well-known at the time. Part of their success was to be forged as a result of this.

The squad must respect their manager and believe in him.

Mutual acceptance of squad and manager didn't present any real obstacles. Benítez had credibility in the dressing room. He earned it without the need to offer concessions. There were no unnecessary displays of firmness, nor excessive generosity to win over devotees to his cause. More important than anything was hard work, and the players grasped this ethos with no problem. Some players in the dressing room already knew him, Cañizares, for example, and others such as Mista and Curro Torres who arrived from Tenerife at the same time as Benítez. The players scrutinised the manager for the first few days without missing a trick, but he acquitted himself well in the test he had been set.

CHOOSING A CAPTAIN

One clear example illustrates who had control of the reins in the dressing room. In the summer of 2003, Benítez played the part of mediator in a thorny issue which needed to be settled before the start of the season. The question of the captaincy.

Who was going to captain Valencia? It might seem an inconsequential issue but at that time it concealed an internal struggle amongst the leading players. The captain needed a certain moral authority, he was responsible for the rest of the players, in short, it was a badge of rank. A symbolic post perhaps, but one with undeniable influence.

In this particular case there was also something else that needed to be decided. At that time Cañizares was acting as captain. His close relationship with the Argentinean players, Aimar, Ayala and Pellegrino made them a group with considerable influence in the dressing room. They were all impressive players. Pellegrino was the member of the group who played least in the first team, but when he did he was almost an extension of the manager when he was out on the pitch. He was the one who best communicated Benítez's instructions. Benítez never concealed his admiration for 'el Flaco' (Pellegrino), and always praised his professionalism and his total dedication, not only on the field but also his understanding and the way in which he lived each game.

The important thing was that the squad couldn't agree on the captaincy for the following season. In the end an unusual voting system was adopted. The ballot box was to be placed in the manager's dressing room. The players would vote but the count and the consequent result would be left solely to Rafa Benítez. No sooner said than done. Everyone agreed.

The voting threw up a change of captain. Baraja and Albelda would share the job being the two with the most votes. Only Benítez knew the exact count, and he has never made it public. It was one of the best kept secrets. It was also one of the conditions that he couldn't disclose it. With Cañizares relieved of his post, a transfer of power took place. These two key elements in the team became the squad's representatives, bringing a different approach to that of the international goalkeeper, though both of the two midfield players were also regulars in the Spanish national team.

The team underperformed for a couple of weeks and had fallen behind the leading group by the end of February. Benítez sent both men a direct message, calling on them to take responsibility and get stuck in. He repeated it in a statement at a press conference so that it would be on the record. The manager asked them to take on the commitment and get more involved. He tightened the rope and it worked. Valencia took off.

Albelda and Baraja responded to the manager's demand although they were surprised by the way in which they received the message. For some time Benítez had wanted the two midfielders to participate more fully in the decisions that affected the team. The change of captaincy suited him because he wanted to win devotees to his cause. He knew too that Cañizares was not going to lose his motivation, quite the opposite, this setback would spur him on to show everyone that he was still the best in goal. So it was, stripped of his armband, the Valencia goalkeeper turned in an excellent season, winning for the fourth time the Ricardo Zamora trophy for the keeper letting in fewest goals in the division.

This issue broke the everyday traditional relationship between squad and coaches. There were other aspects of everyday practice, which by virtue of repetition became routine. Preparation for a game followed an unchangeable ritual other than in a few exceptional cases. Benítez was never keen on long pre-match base camps. On the eve of home matches the team would gather in the late afternoon at a hotel. At first it was the Parador Luis Vives in El Saler. Later, because of refurbishment, they moved to a hotel closer to the sports complex at Paterna. Both enabled gentle workouts to take place at suitable facilities on match day.

In his final phase as manager of Valencia, Benítez abolished the evening pre-match sessions before home fixtures, preferring to bring the first team players together to train first thing in the morning. Then they would go to the hotel for lunch and afterwards to the ground. Players had dinner and spent the night before the game at home. A decision that conveyed his confidence in the players' habits and in their professionalism. It was originally adopted because of the crowded fixture calendar when League games come together with games in Europe. This subjected the squad to a constant to-ing and fro-ing. It was a way of making rest and recovery easier.

Preparation for a game followed an unchangeable ritual.

When travelling, the routine was the same although it included the journey. The closest were done by coach, those over 250 miles by plane. For some years now Valencia has chartered a plane which makes travel to away fixtures easier and avoids formalities. Less time is lost because schedules are adapted to the needs of the team. There are no stopovers on the way and flights prove financially cost-effective.

On some occasions, Benítez showed his dissatisfaction with the organisation of the travel arrangements. For a League match in Zaragoza during the 2003-04 season, the team travelled by road although the manager had wanted to go by plane to save time as Valencia were playing in the UEFA

Cup that week. His request was denied, which made him angry. At the start of that season, while speaking in public, he slipped in a remark about the wisdom of travelling to Barcelona by plane as 48 hours later they were to play a Cup game in Castellón. Again he wasn't successful.

It wasn't that he was particularly keen on air travel. He was well aware of the major drawback of never-ending waits at airports, but he always wanted his point of view to be taken into account. This is one of his most striking traits: an irrepressible tendency to want to be involved in every issue and always to give his opinion – even in matters that are, strictly speaking, outside his jurisdiction. He likes to control everything.

It was not only ice cream that caused problems.

On the other hand though, Benítez doesn't keep a tight check on the lives of his players, nor does he phone them at ungodly hours to check whether they are at home. This is a practice undertaken by other managers, one which has become very entrenched.

Initially at Valencia a rule was drawn up that obliged players to be home no later than eleven. After talks with the squad's representatives greater flexibility was granted. Work demands nowadays are so great that a player finds this out for himself after a wild night out. The training sessions give them away and Benítez can tell if any player has been overdoing it.

He has a general awareness of the private life of each player and there is no lack of casual informants to pass on the relevant information if anything untoward is detected. Of course, a certain degree of flexibility is allowed. A tacit understanding allows for nights out after matches, provided that the work schedule doesn't demand a period of rest. In turn, the squad would usually organise a series of dinners over the season after which they would visit a nightclub. This issue, which on occasion can cause tension, usually settles over time as the players and manager get to know each other better and either takes on greater importance or goes unnoticed depending on the performance on the pitch.

ICE CREAM WARS

Benítez kept strict control of the players' diets. Menus were agreed with, and supervised by the club doctor, Jordi Candel. They would contain basic ingredients such as pasta, salads, grilled meat or fish, lots of fruit and yoghurt. Sauces were out. This was the range of food, similar to that of all professional teams, that the Valencia squad ate on match days, on the eve of matches and after matches.

However there were some matters of disagreement.

One of the first serious problems that Benítez faced at Valencia related to the players' nutrition. The removal of ordinary ice cream from the players' diet led to a strong reaction from the players against him. The intention had been to replace it with ice cream made from skimmed milk, which has a composition recommended for top-class sportsmen because it contains no fat. The disagreement became public knowledge and there were considerable repercussions. Benítez was particularly annoyed because it was presented as a complete ban when in fact it was only a modification, and because the story had been leaked from the dressing room. Some players refused to accept the recommendation and one of them, Kily González, even had a heated argument over it.

A RICE PADDY

It was not only ice cream that caused problems.

A ban on rice as part of the players' diet during pre-match training camps was also announced. There were some dissenting voices in the squad. They argued that in the past Valencia had achieved excellent performances with this in their regular diet. A meeting was even held with Dr Candel to call for an explanation. Benítez fully backed the doctor.

From early on in the Ranieri era the players had been used to eating mildly seasoned rice with vegetables and scarcely any meat when they were at the Parador in El Saler on evening match days. Whilst the dish was called paella the recipe was in fact closer to risotto milanese. Some players hadn't digested their food properly and for this reason it was the doctor who had taken the initiative to remove the dish. Benítez gave him his wholehearted support. Yet these were his first months at the club and Benítez harboured the fear that this issue would gain him not only the opposition of some of his players, but also public ill-will, given the rice-growing tradition of Valencia. And he was upset at the way the matter had been presented.

In the end though, rice wasn't removed from the menu, instead its seasoning was changed and, from then on, it was only served boiled. The storm that had been caused by this measure took a while to subside and it achieved great notoriety at the time. Inevitably Rafa Benítez's image suffered some damage with the public.

There were other restrictions. For instance, olives were not considered good for the players' diet, and onion and tuna fish were removed from salads on match days. Fizzy drinks were not allowed either.

But not everything was banned. Moderate amounts of wine could be consumed. One bottle per table. Some players liked wine with their meals, whilst others never even touched it. The players that drank wine usually only had a glass and the bottles were never left more than half empty. Wine is an anti-oxidant recommended in moderation by many doctors and not viewed as diminishing sporting performance – good quality wines were always chosen.

Both the manager and the doctor were in agreement on other issues which they deemed fundamental, such as monitoring a player's recovery after a game. Correct nutrition and the consumption of carbohydrates are essential because of their energy-releasing properties.

After each game the players were given a ready-made drink rich in carbohydrates and a plate of various fruits. Sometimes, on return trips after matches, a light dinner of sandwiches would be rustled up, to speed things up and get everyone back home quickly. There is a particular story which is worth telling.

Valencia were already League Champions and were preparing for the UEFA Cup Final. One Friday they were playing at Villarreal. The game, an unimportant one for the Mestalla team, kicked off at ten o'clock at night. Rafa Benítez and the team doctor agreed that it was advisable to stop on their way back for dinner at a hotel.

The suggestion didn't go down well with the players. Most of them wanted to get home for dinner – they were close to Valencia, only a little over forty minutes away, a comfortably short motorway journey. Benítez and the doctor had taken the decision to ensure the proper recovery of the players. They were well aware that there was no guarantee that, once home, all the footballers would eat the food that was recommended after a match. That uncertainty, close to an important final, persuaded them to make a decision that was unpopular with the squad. The late hour, one in the morning, and the fact that some players lived alone and didn't have a well-stocked larder, strengthened the appropriateness of their decision. The players didn't like the manager being so meticulous, but it was the right thing to do. Had they been allowed to do what they wanted, it's probable that some players would have grabbed anything they could in Valencia and wouldn't have followed the doctor's suggestions.

It was not only the food that the coach kept his eye on.

But it was not only the food that the coach kept his eye on, but also who sat with whom at meal times. It was always instructive to see who was sitting at which table. In this way, the personal friendships and incompatibilities which exist in any squad could be seen. These complex relations were also reflected in the way rooms were allocated. There were players who wanted the privacy of single rooms, but Benítez always kept to his custom of dividing the players into pairs in twin rooms.

Each pair was chosen according to either their personal compatibility or their position on the pitch. Sometimes it was important that players who were to share similar roles on the pitch were put together – an approach Benítez had adopted during his time at Extremadura.

Benítez believed in analysing the game with his squad in the morning but he never took advantage of this preparation time to announce his line-up. Over the three seasons he maintained his practice of including a video session in which he used images to point out the most prominent aspects of their opponents' play. This run-through never lasted more than an hour and the pictures had been edited to highlight the most important tactical points of their opponents. Benítez never showed a complete game but rather summarised it and explained all the factors to be borne in mind.

The players received carefully edited information; they only had to grasp the essential points. The coaches had broken down the opponent's system beforehand and cut out all the trivial aspects. The video machine ended up being yet another travelling companion and, so as to avoid the costs of hiring one from hotels, Valencia always included it on their trips. At this technical pep talk the players would listen and on a few occasions contribute. Everything would be sorted out at this meeting before lunch, although the players were only made aware of their inclusion in the team once they reached the ground and the pitch had been inspected.

The reason for this approach was to keep the players motivated as long as possible, right up to the start of the match. If a player knew in the morning that he was on the substitutes' bench there was a risk that he would become disheartened, and that his mood could affect the general atmosphere. Players usually sense whether they are going to be included or not in the starting line-up but, as Benítez isn't one of those managers given to constant repetition in his team selections, they are never totally sure until they have heard confirmation from the manager's mouth. On more than one occasion he has changed line-ups which looked like foregone conclusions and caused surprises in the dressing room. In this way a player has less time to think about it and take in the disappointment of not making the team.

Rafa Benítez used to write down all these details in his notebook. Although the Dutchman Van Gaal became famous for the diary notes he wrote during games, it isn't commonly known that Benítez did the same. It went everywhere with him and he entered any detail that he considered important. Unlike the former Barça manager he didn't show it off to people, but it was inseparable from him. He didn't want to forget anything and so he wrote it down. Later he transferred it all to his computer, on which every day-to-day matter, however trivial it may seem, is now meticulously recorded.

In his dealings with footballers Benítez always kept his distance, though his position in the hierarchy didn't save him from sometimes being the butt of his players' pranks. At times players are not averse to create embarrassing situations. On more than one occasion the match day meal was at the same time as the sports news. As they and the coaching staff sat there they would watch Benítez appearing on screen to make his pre-match comments, and this would give rise to hissing and the odd amusing comment. Smiles could be seen on some faces and the situation became relaxed. This informality didn't stop respect from being shown at pre-match meetings. Rafa Benítez, although he maintained his habitual seriousness, took these practical jokes in the best possible way.

THE CHAMPIONSHIP RETURNS TO MESTALLA

"I think we can do great things, I like what I see, there are great possibilities."

Rafa Benítez is not a man given to boasting or hollow rhetoric; he's not usually a man to say something unless he believes it. During his first summer as manager of Valencia, this was the message that he gave to those closest to him.

Initially his signing had caused reticence but this had now evaporated. Having been given the opportunity, he was also being given the benefit of the doubt. For the vast majority of fans he was still an unknown although they liked the way that he talked about his football plan. It was clear and well argued, and he didn't brag. He worked with his usual team and planned the season meticulously. Subirats brought him up-to-date although he arrived at Valencia with first-hand information. He believed in his squad. His work soon began to bear fruit. The squad absorbed his style and adapted to his methods. They began to understand each other. Benítez found himself among a good-natured group used to competing at the highest level, committed to sacrifice and eager to fight for titles with excellent footballing skills and a great sense of professionalism.

The team had followed a consistent path over the previous three years. Ranieri and Cúper, his predecessors, had given it a distinct personality. Nevertheless, their qualities still hadn't shone through. Their potential could bring new triumphs. Benítez knew it; he had watched all the videos and knew each and every one of the players inside out.

Day to day dealings confirmed his intuition. Along with his inseparable fitness trainer, Paco Ayestarán, he took on, as his assistant coach, Antonio

López, whom he knew well and who would prove to be an excellent ally on this journey. He also added José Manuel Ochotorena to his team of co-workers as goalkeeper coach. His lengthy experience as goalkeeper for several teams – including those of the stature of Real Madrid and Valencia – took him in his day to the Spanish national team. He knew his job and the club and would be of great service. He joined them somewhat hurriedly. The person first chosen had been the former goalkeeper, Sempere, a man who had spent fifteen seasons with Valencia, but who, in the end, turned the job down.

The first setback shook the foundations of the club. The resignation of the chairman, Pedro Cortés, who had signed him on, was the final consequence of the traumatic departure of Gaizka Mendieta, the talismatic player par excellence, their captain, their symbol over the last few years and someone who represented the breakthrough of Valencia into the limelight of football.

PRESSURE ON THE BOARD

The departure of Mendieta led to great debate. All indications pointed to him going to Real Madrid, but in the end massive popular pressure diverted him to Lazio. The famous *rat penat* (winged rat) on the coat of arms flew far away from Mestalla, and Cortés had no other option than to stick to the promise he had given in front of 50,000 fans at his last presentation. "No important player will leave Valencia while I am chairman. If they go I will resign," he had said angrily after the departure of Fariños, Gerard and Claudio López.

He handed over to vice-chairman Jaume Ortí with tears in his eyes. Benítez knew what he was getting himself into. He observed events from a safe distance; he went his own way. He worried more about football matters than these wars behind closed doors. He had only just arrived at the club when the chairman and the captain left. He had met Mendieta at the first training sessions but he knew the player intented to leave Valencia. He simply accepted it, sticking to his belief that he wasn't interested in relying on a player, whoever it might be, whose heart was not in the job – and Mendieta's certainly wasn't.

The change in chairman didn't affect his job in the slightest. He would deal with the most immediate professional matters with other officials, but he

Rafa Benítez with Jaume Ortí (centre) and Jesús Garcia Pitarch.

was to find in the new man at the top someone who was open-minded, cooperative and willing to discuss matters. Besides, Valencia was a club which, over the last few years, had become used to internal upheavals of this kind. Since it had been forced to convert to a PLC such occurrences had become everyday affairs, with only the occasional lull. These storms didn't have the slightest effect on the sporting achievements of the club, quite the opposite, they weren't influenced by these internecine struggles and, after winning the Cup in 1999, Valencia's progress was unstoppable.

Having accepted the reality of the situation, Benítez got down to planning the season. The matter of reinforcements was the stormiest issue. Marchena came from Benfica in exchange for Zahovic's departure; Rufete and De los Santos, from Málaga; Salva, from Atlético Madrid; and two men who had been with him at Tenerife, Curro Torres and Mista. The most expensive signings, De los Santos and Salva, would be the crosses he would have to bear. Their cost was close to £20m.

One strand of opinion reproached him for these signings – and their absence in the line-ups would later speak for itself. Valencia had Sergio within reach, the winger from Espanyol. He was a more attacking and virtuoso player than De los Santos but Benítez needed a replacement for Albelda and so leaned towards the Uruguayan midfielder. Salva came to the club having been the top goal scorer in the first division with Racing Santander, as well as in the second division with Atlético in the previous two seasons. It seemed a guarantee. Later, he was to become a problem. Benítez's quarrels with the striker were obvious. Benítez demanded work and specific moves based on a planned approach, whilst Salva did his own thing, fighting, running and struggling on his own, chasing goals with an anarchical verve – almost obsessively. The two were just not in tune with each other and this was to be a constant for the whole time they were together.

A NEW SEASON BEGINS

The fixture list brought them a daunting start to the season for the second year running. Once again Valencia and Real Madrid faced each other in the opening game, this time at Mestalla. The match was fraught. It might have been Benítez's debut, but he was eclipsed by Zidane. The Valencia manager gladly conceded the limelight, but studied Zidane's style of play thoroughly. Now nicknamed "the Galacticos" because of their accumulation of star players, Madrid arrived at Valencia's ground in their centenary year ready to conquer the world.

The Madrid sports press had spent all summer singing the praises of the team managed by Del Bosque. It was a red-letter season. The inclusion of the French midfielder unleashed euphoria amongst their most ardent fans. All eyes were on the brilliant stars of Real Madrid. Valencia, despite being the home team, seemed almost to be an uninvited guest at the party, and bristled at having to take on this secondary role.

In this atmosphere, and with Mestalla ready to provide the appropriate response, a fantastically tense game followed. Valencia played better and scored early. Madrid weren't at ease on the pitch; they found it difficult to develop any pattern of play. The match became heated and Figo was sent off.

Madrid demanded the same treatment for Albelda for his marking of Zidane. It was the first chapter in a battle that would continue throughout the season and which would have critical moments. Benítez had won the game; he couldn't have had a better start. His men had won by the narrowest of margins. This most sought after victory gave Valencia hope. Those who had mistrusted the manager, sitting on the bench for the first time, now gave him their vote of confidence, recognising his maturity and the wisdom of his strategy.

The path through the championship from that initial match would lead Valencia to the top end of the table. They weren't dazzling but they weren't showing signs of weakness either. They were reliable at home and came away from prestigious settings, such as San Mamés and Nou Camp with creditable draws, in both cases scoring two goals. At both showdowns they dominated throughout but victory evaded them at the last moment, especially at Bilbao, where they had had a comfortable lead of 2-0. Athletic responded in the final minutes with characteristic spirit and put two past the keeper.

Aimar had already left the pitch after having given a magnificent performance. This substitution was interpreted by the media as an example of excessive confidence on the part of the manager. The veiled criticisms rained down on Benítez for this substitution which some thought hasty. The games went by and, despite Valencia being on top and the only team in the first division not to have suffered a defeat, the atmosphere began to heat up. The pressure began to build as a result of both some dull matches and some close ones, such as the one against Rayo at home. The fans always want more.

Some of the media gave them no respite and waited for their first slip and the opportunity to unleash all their pent-up criticisms. The moment soon arrived. The team were overwhelmed. Five matches without a win and only one goal scored. The first defeat, against Real Sociedad, undoubtedly turned the tables. The noose was tightening and the outlook was worrying.

THE PRESSURE MOUNTS

Valencia lost ground and slipped down the table. Benítez was going through his most precarious period. His critics joined the fray, proclaiming that they had seen it coming, and unashamedly pronouncing that the coach wasn't up to managing a team of that stature. This climate of doubt spread as far as the club directors, who became nervous and considered taking urgent action. Benítez was aware of the gravity of the situation.

By half-time it all seemed wrapped up and Benítez's survival in the job in serious doubt.

The first fillip came at the beginning of December in Glasgow when the team won a very tough UEFA Cup qualifying round against Celtic in a penalty shoot-out. However, the improvement they yearned for in the League did not come, and the mood of the team was depressed. Against this backdrop came the last outing of 2001. Barcelona was the destination. Here they were to face Espanyol, on a ground on which they seemed to have been doomed since time immemorial. Valencia had lost three consecutive Cup finals in the mid 40s at the Olímpico de Montjuic and, since it had been the home ground of Espanyol, Valencia had always lost except for once in the Intertoto.

Benítez's future as manager was at stake. It would be an unforgettable night for all sorts of reasons. It was the match that marked the turning point, and from it, the team which would end up League Champions, would emerge heartened.

On the eve of the match they knew it was going to be a different sort of game. The city of Barcelona and a sizeable part of the Mediterranean coastline had suffered heavy snowfall. Everyday life was affected: traffic in the streets was at a standstill, the traffic lights weren't working, roads were closed, lots of people were cut off. It was chaos. The storm had caught the Valencia team on the motorway and their coach arrived in Barcelona with great difficulty, and very late. Some thought was given to postponing the match.

On the Saturday morning a pitch inspection was carried out and it was declared fit for play. The temperature stood at around zero, there was a risk of snowfall at the beginning of the match and some snow did actually fall. Transport links with Valencia had been suspended and some directors, journalists and fans who had planned to go to Barcelona had to turn back because the roads had been closed.

The match was played in front of a scant crowd of 5,000 on the freezing terraces. The clash started off in a discouraging fashion for Valencia, who weren't up to scratch, letting in two goals in the first half.

By half time it all seemed wrapped up and Benítez's survival in the job in serious doubt. He was more out than in, and not just him but also Subirats, the man who had stood up for Benítez. With nothing to lose, Valencia appealed to heroism for the second half. There has been much speculation as to what happened during half time at that legendary match but all those involved insist there was nothing special, nothing extraordinary. There was an appeal to go all out for the game, that there was time left, and they had to try to recover. There was no haranguing from the manager or anything like that. And just one substitution, Aimar was replaced in the second half by Mista.

In scarcely twenty minutes the game completely turned around. Valencia scored three goals and could have got more. Their opponents now seemed to be as frozen as the brave spectators who had defied such a diabolical night. For the first time at Montjuic, the magical Barcelona mountain made the Mestalla club happy.

BACK ON COURSE?

Amazingly everything changed that night. Valencia gained their first away victory of the season, they scored more than two goals in a match, their manager began to recover his lost credibility and it was the start of a good spell for the team. Victories followed one after another; the team was perking up and began its fight back for the title. The visit to the Bernabéu, at the start of the second half of the season, was beginning to look a really thrilling prospect.

The Real Madrid-Valencia match didn't disappoint. For Rafa Benítez it had a special significance; he was returning to what had been home. On the other bench sat Vicente del Bosque, with whom he had worked closely. Now fate brought them face to face and there was no place for friendship. From that game on the relationship between them would cool. The Madrid supporters were out for revenge for what had happened on the opening day of the season. The atmosphere was tense. They had it in for Valencia but the team from Mestalla weren't daunted and handled themselves well.

The refereeing was the determining factor. The game was presided over by Pérez Pérez, from the Canary Islands. He wasn't one of the top referees and was overwhelmed by the magnitude of the fixture. In the first half a goal by the Romanian Ilie was disallowed for a non-existent offside. Some of the Madrid defenders, especially Hierro, acted with total impunity. It was as if the referee didn't dare to send him off. Albelda's play on the other hand was being put under the microscope, though the midfielder didn't commit a single foul, though he did nearly score with a shot from close to the halfway line. Madrid won by the narrowest of margins, but that was far from the last to be heard of the contest. A bitter controversy was brewing. For the Valencia supporters the game was little short of daylight robbery.

In the post-match press conference, Benítez appeared depressed. He didn't hold back. He was incandescent with rage, branding the defeat unfair. The chairman of Valencia announced that it seemed to him that it had been decreed that Madrid should win the League because they were celebrating their centenary that year. This was vehemently rebuffed. Hostilities broke out in the media circles of both clubs. In Valencia they closed ranks around the Mestalla club, which was unusual because until then the Valencian press had only been hostile to Barcelona.

With such a turbulent scene the team went to pieces suffering its only defeat of the season a week later at home. This was against Valladolid, the only visiting team to score more than a single goal – one an own goal and the other the result of a monumental series of defensive errors. It was an ill-fated afternoon for Valencia. The extent to which the players had lost focus was clear, as was the emotional toll that was being paid for what had happened in the Bernabéu.

At that point, Benítez played a winning card. The team had fallen apart and needed a *coup de théâtre* to regain their spirits and believe in their own abilities again. This message was also addressed to their entourage. If the uproar in the news had been counterproductive after the game against 'you know who', then the manager was going to turn things around by appearing voluntarily before the media.

WE CAN WIN THE LEAGUE

His press conference was unplanned and he surprised the journalists who came to the Paterna premises. His speech was simple, contradicting what the chairman and other directors had said, he stated that the League could be won, that there was still time and that the team were capable of it. His tone was confident. He made no reference to refereeing but asked for the support of the fans because he believed it to be vital. The message, full of optimism, produced the desired effect. It was the eve of their match against one of the top teams of the championship, Athletic Bilbao. It would be the first victory of three against other illustrious teams such as Barça and Sevilla who were to lose at Mestalla in unmitigated disasters. As if by magic, the situation had changed and Benítez's forecast came true. The strategy drawn up together with the club press officer, Jordi Bruixola, had been the correct one. Valencia went into the lead on winning at Alavés' ground in a strange game. The players from Vitoria scored in the first minute. In the following one came the equaliser, then a little later the winning goal. They were the work of De los Santos and Carew who hadn't managed a goal until that night. Almost at the end of the clash a penalty for the home team was saved by Cañizares. It had been thirty-one years since Valencia had been top in the second half of the league season.

As if by magic, the situation had changed and Benítez's forecast came true.

The game at Mendizorroza was a joke compared to the visit by Osasuna. The Valencians enjoyed the luck of champions in a heart-stopping contest. Valencia missed a penalty in the first half and the Navarre team lost a man through a sending-off. Osasuna played with only ten men but resisted strongly and even had a golden opportunity at 0-0 in the second half, miraculously missed by Djukic. Immediately afterwards Valencia scored. Shortly after, Osasuna equalised. In injury time a defender made a goal line clearance to stop Osasuna scoring and in the next move Baraja, who had missed the Valencia penalty, scored the winning goal. The stadium erupted, the supporters could not believe their eyes. Luck shone that day on a Valencia team traumatised from having been knocked out of the UEFA Cup by Inter Milan three days earlier. Inter had been forced to put an outfield player into goal after their keeper Toldo had been sent off when they'd already used all their substitutes. Valencia had several opportunities to score, but failed.

That afternoon, against Osasuna, Benítez rested some members of the first-team who had played against Inter, even though the terraces chanted for them, especially Aimar, given the way the game was turning out. Amid frayed tempers and great tension the match was salvaged, and the manager was left with a positive conclusion: the pairing of central defenders Marchena and Djukic was more suitable for home games than that of the usual Argentine one of Pellegrino and Ayala, whose ability to clear balls played from behind was limited.

The Valencia-Madrid title contest became more acute with Deportivo on their heels in the final stages of the season. No-one gave way. Valencia beat Tenerife through a stunning goal by Aimar; then thrashed Real Sociedad and drew in Majorca, a draw which meant little but which had great value 24 hours later when Madrid were beaten in Pamplona.

Sentence was passed on the League with the two consecutive victories by Benítez's men at Mestalla, both of which were dramatic games. Both clashes were decided by the narrowest of margins. The Deportivo match was won with a scrappy goal, due in part to the cunning of Aimar and in part to the misfortune of Duscher, who beat his own goalkeeper. The explosion came against Espanyol. As in the first half of the season this match was the decisive one.

This time there was no snow, and the temperature up on the terraces amongst the fans was high. Real Madrid were playing in San Sebastián. Aware of the importance of their fixture, the hunger to win became the worst enemy for Benítez's men.

In this duel, the manager really did have to make an effort in the interval to rescue the team from the state of uncontrolled agitation they found

Valencia celebrate winning La Liga under Rafa Benítez

themselves in and get them back on track. They found themselves one down at half-time, following a penalty after an absurd piece of play. Carboni had been sent off after losing his temper and elbowing an opponent. Things couldn't have been worse although Valencia had created a number of chances to score.

The dressing room therapy consisted of positively channelling the nervous energy of the players away from panic and towards the achievement of an intensity of play, which would crush their rivals. That's how it happened. Valencia cornered Espanyol and achieved supremacy despite being a man down. In fact, it looked as if it was the other team who had ten men. Play was deep in the Espanyol half; you could see the goal coming but it never arrived. The news from Anoeta lifted the home crowd, Real Sociedad had scored at almost the same time as Valencia drew level at Mestalla.

THE CHAMPIONSHIP BECKONS

In the midst of all the general uproar, the austere and contained figure of the manager could be seen. His concentration was firmly on his team's recovery not being spoilt at the last minute. Not a single gesture of jubilation. His team had drained themselves, their motivation had led to a performance well beyond themselves; they had broken through that mysterious barrier of teams that refuse to give up until they have achieved their objective. Once again, it was another emotive comeback that coincided with the defeat of Real Madrid in San Sebastián.

Valencia now felt that they were the champions, their overwhelming display left no room for doubt. The story had ended like a screen thriller. Not even Hitchcock, the master of the genre, could have dreamt up a better plot. That night the Championship was virtually wrapped up. And for Valencia, it was more than just a straightforward result. It was confirmation of their strength – the final acid test. That first Sunday in May 2002, Valencia were proclaimed League Champions after defeating Malaga at home with two first half goals.

Nothing gets past Rafa, though he likes to read too much into everything.

And there was still one week to go to the end of the season.

Thirty-one years had passed since Valencia's last League title. But the outcome had already been decided the week earlier. The match at La Rosaleda, that 5th May, was a mere formality. Benítez knew it was over. The workmanship his men had shown in Malaga had killed off any vestige of hope for the others. The crowning ceremony was staged with exuberant joy, there were no obstacles left in the way. Rafa Benítez had sensed the possibilities in the loneliness of the summer base camp in Holland.

It hadn't been a gratuitous comment.

"This year we can do great things."

FLEETING HAPPINESS

The day after winning the League it rained heavily in Valencia. But this didn't stop the Valencia supporters going out into the streets to celebrate winning the title. It was a festive day and thousands of people defied the rain. The flood of water and people left indelible memories of happiness as the Champions were welcomed home.

The team flew in just after noon and the celebrations lasted well into the night. The team followed the traditional route reserved for these occasions; visiting the basilica of the Virgen de los Desamparados; the Generalitat palace, where a massive lunch was laid on; and City Hall. The final chapter was played out at the Mestalla stadium.

Benítez accepted an invitation to go to the Valencian regional television studios along with the club chairman, Jaume Ortí. It was the culmination of a marathon day. They both arrived at the last minute and with their clothes wringing wet. They were given a dressing room while they dried their clothes, and raced into make-up five minutes before the start of the programme.

Benítez's fatigue could be seen in his face. He had scarcely slept and his replies had lost their sparkle. He was tired of interviews. He only reacted when faced with a report in which the players in the squad appeared, one by one, to a different musical accompaniment reflecting their role in the conquest of the title. Each player had his song, some of which exuded a certain irony. The content surprised him and he showed his disagreement with some of the melodies chosen – though only a minority – or with the pictures selected. Once again his perfectionist streak shone through.

Nothing gets past Rafa, though he likes to read too much into everything. It was the only diversion from the expected discussion. Everything was running smoothly and there was a restrained elation. Now was not the time to be a wet blanket; the party had already been subjected to a downpour. Now it was time to respect the immense enjoyment of the fans. Benítez doesn't give free rein to his feelings, his satisfaction is always restrained, he thinks about the future. When the studio lights were dimmed he would express himself with discomfiting sincerity.

The programme came to an end and Benítez made his way along the corridors of Canal Nou, eager to return home and regain some peace and quiet. He was on his own. While the chairman left quickly with Jordi Bruixola, chief press officer, to go to a celebration dinner, Rafa preferred to go home. His car was parked in the sports centre in Paterna. I took him in mine. Toni Peris, the Head of Sports Productions, went with us. On the way, just a short journey of five minutes or so, Rafa started a monologue which I hardly dared interrupt. It was a volcano. All the pent-up tension – the problems negotiated, the difficulties experienced – streamed out of him. He spoke energetically, with no bitterness and in a constructive vein. He was worried about the future. There was no room for complacency or for any self-satisfaction in the success he had achieved. He didn't bask in the glory.

Scarcely twenty-four hours later and in a different location Rafa was yet again expressing his fears for the following season. There was absolute sincerity. He felt the urgent need for the team to defend the title and to once again participate in the Champions League. He wasn't fazed by the challenge but there were internal issues that troubled him. To listen to him, no-one would have believed that here was the manager of the Valencia team which had won the Spanish league for the first time in three decades.

Our conversation lasted half an hour. Thirty intense minutes with me listening in absolute silence. In the solitude of the premises where the daily toil of the Champions had been hammered out, Benítez told me of his concerns. That memorable chat could be summed up as his recognition of one pressing need: Valencia had to have a competitive spirit in the squad, the players couldn't be allowed to snuggle down and become complacent after a triumph of this scale. Time was to prove him right. His diagnosis was accurate. The euphoria gave way to a hangover, and then to an excess of confidence. He feared that the squad would rest on their laurels, and wouldn't maintain the intense work rate which had taken them to glory. The attitude of some of the players was reason for special concern.

Certain players really worried him: Kily González and Salva, in particular. The Argentinean had shown himself to be vital in the final stretch of the Championship. His appearances had made the difference at key moments but there was no guarantee of consistency. The striker didn't appear at meetings, nor was he expected to any longer. A disturbing case, but a player who Benítez himself had insisted on signing.

This negativity could affect the group. And so it was vital to look for new signings, and bring in new faces. Ahead lay a long summer; a World Cup in an exotic location and, despite the financial constraints, the chance to find reinforcements in Korea and Japan. Events would unfold however in the opposite direction to his wishes. The club could not shake off the euphoria of winning the title.

Another contributory factor, which prevented the search for signings so longed for by the manager, was the split between the Director of Sport, Javier Subirats, and the Chief Executive, Manuel Llorente. And some of those at the heart of Valencia felt there was no need to strengthen the team.

Everyone went their separate ways. Benítez commentated on some of the World Cup games. Javier Subirats, who now knew that he was more out of the club than in it, also acted as a commentator. With the threat hanging over his head and the lack of sufficient finance, Subirats' enthusiasm for scouring the football market was scant. Valencia didn't make any signings in the summer of 2002.

It was a far from healthy atmosphere. The lack of harmony between the club executives led to an unremitting tension which was conveyed to the fans by the media. The first warning of internal instability surfaced when Valencia were thrashed in the Spanish Super Cup by Deportivo La Coruña. They lost in both legs. First there was a collapse at Riazor, then a failed comeback at Mestalla with a final aggregate score of 4-0, as significant as it was worrying.

Having gone through a bad patch, one had the feeling that there was a determination to improve. Benítez was expecting a reaction from the squad

Benítez took drastic action and sent the players back to the dressing room.

and that the debacle against Deportivo would act as an incentive. It didn't turn out that way. The situation took on a disquieting complexion on the eve of their debut in the 2002-03 League season. Valencia were playing their first game at San Moix against Majorca.

That Saturday, during the final training session, something unusual took place which surprised the journalists who were watching the progress of the players. Not long after the start of the session Benítez took drastic action and sent the players back to the dressing room. They had been out for scarcely fifteen minutes. Confusion was rife. Reporters swarmed around outside where the players and the manager were to emerge. They were impatient for news.

The players came out looking rather glum. They played it down and dodged the issue with diplomatic replies. The manager was more explicit. He confirmed the suspicions and used the presence of the press to pass his message to the fans. He was straight to the point:

"I've suspended the training session because the players aren't motivated or showing the attitude I think they should adopt."

Benítez was irate. It was time to fire a warning shot at the players, there was still a chance to change course. The symptoms worried him, he knew his men only too well and could see that they had lowered their sights. The performance of a group depends on getting the maximum contribution from each and everyone of its members. If they weren't going all out, they would fail to defend the title. The decision to suspend that training session was questioned, and some saw it as no more than a theatrical gesture.

The team must work flat out if it wants to achieve its targets.

Benítez's reaction was deliberate. The apathy of the players annoyed him deeply, and added to his reservations of which the players had been unaware. They had always trusted in their ability to pull it off in games and they didn't suffer the anguish which torments managers before a game. In the dressing room after that failed session, there was no meeting, nor was the matter discussed. There was a pretence of normality though things were far from normal.

Benítez didn't consider it the right moment to force the situation. He was waiting for the players to get the message and for them to rise to the challenge that the imminent start to the season would bring. He had thrown down the gauntlet, he was impugning their honour as Champions. Now he expected a response from a team whose pride had been wounded. Hours later the squad would meet in Paterna before leaving for the airport where a plane would take them to Majorca for the first match of the season. It was a convincing performance, a clear 2-0 win with goals by De los Santos and Baraja. Valencia projected an image of seriousness as they had done when they had won the title. There was no showiness and there were no weaknesses. The question was inevitable: Was the victory a consequence of what had happened the day before? The team played the matter down and made little of the manager's controversial decision. Their evasive answers were their way of saying that they didn't need those measures to give their all on the pitch, although deep down some of them really just wanted to shut up the manager.

Rafa Benítez didn't want to rub salt in the wound and so he didn't link the two events. But he did reassert his maxim that 'the team must work flat out if it wants to achieve its targets'. Subliminally, he persisted in his demand that they apply themselves if they wanted to be at their most competitive. It wouldn't be the last time that he would address the squad and demand that they improve their attitude.

The next time would be at a rowdy press conference that shook the club to its foundations. It was the eve of the qualifier for the semi-finals of the Champions League against Inter Milan at Mestalla. The season was coming into its final straight. Valencia had had some ups-and-downs but had kept their hopes alive in the two most important competitions: the Spanish League and the Champions League. In the League they were in the leading pack and still hoped to break the historic curse which had always seemed to stop them holding on to the title for a second year. During the winter they had strung together a series of important wins, amongst them a feast of goals at the Nou Camp, despite having been a man down from the first half. And now the Three Kings (the Spanish version of Father Christmas) had brought them their Christmas present – the winger they had longed for. The Frenchman, Reivellere, joined in the winter transfer window, a versatile and classy footballer.

Now they had the chance to repeat their celebrations of the previous year. The team fought to overcome the embarrassment of possible elimination in the second group phase of the Champions League. They would gamble everything against an old adversary, Arsenal. It was the special day of 19th March, the feast of St Joseph, the main day of the local fiesta, las Fallas, and with all this going on Mestalla never fails. The match lived up to expectations and Valencia became Arsenal's *bête noire*, winning by two goals. There were wild celebrations on the terraces and Benítez began to look to the future with confidence.

One month later and the storm clouds were gathering. Progress in the League came to a screeching halt and the chance of the title vanished. Attention was now focused on Europe. At home, Valencia needed to overturn a 1-0 deficit from the first leg against one of their bogey sides, Inter Milan. The return of the former Valencia manager, Cúper, also stirred up old demons but Benítez outdid everyone the day before the encounter. Again, he let loose a withering harangue in front of surprised journalists, in particular the Italian press.

"There are players with no drive and they contaminate the rest of the team. You need enthusiasm. There are players who work but the problem is that they only do so now and again. To sun ourselves, have a good time and end up finishing between fourth or sixth in the league, we'll get by, but if we aspire to better things we must rekindle our enthusiasm every day, we must get our feet wet if we want to be champions again."

These verbal missiles, aimed at a section of his squad, upset the atmosphere before the match.

"We've got a couple of months to put up with each other," was the finishing touch to the outburst from an indignant manager. Benítez was desperate. His team knew the symptoms but made no effort to find a remedy. Amedeo Carboni had diagnosed it days earlier: "After winning the League we aren't as hungry as we were a year ago."

The squad were divided over this. One sector agreed and applauded Carboni, others considered that he shouldn't have said it even though it was right; then there were the dissidents who didn't agree with the content and, even less, with the way it had been announced.

The next day there was a game, and it was a good one. The tension was palpable, but over and above the hostility there was the chance to reach the semi-finals of the Champions League for the third time in four years. In this match they needed to beat Inter 2-0. The storyline was to be cruelly repeated. The Italians went into the lead very early after a monumental defensive error. Nevertheless, Valencia clawed their way back and began to play well. Aimar didn't take long to equalise. The fans roared their approval and the atmosphere at Mestalla was that of one of the great nights. The pressure became asphyxiating, Inter retreated into their half but then came the goal by Baraja and the stadium erupted. There was still time to qualify. A foul by Materazzi on Sánchez was a clear penalty but the referee didn't give it. Valencia pushed forward relentlessly but Inter stood their ground as best they could in an agonising final period.

When Benítez arrived at the press room that night he praised his men's performance and openly attacked the speculative style of their opponents, both the ends and the means of achieving it. Again Inter, as in the previous year, had got there without deserving it, leaving Valencia out of Europe after they had given it their all. The return to harsh reality wasn't easy. The open wounds on the eve of the game didn't heal and relations between the manager and part of the squad had been seriously damaged. The rift was obvious. With these ingredients the outcome was predictable, Valencia were in a spin. They lost their fourth place in the League and dropped out of Champions League contention.

No-one could imagine at that time, as the stifling summer of 2003 began, that the best season in Valencia's history was about to be written.

Rafa **BENÍTEZ**

>> CHAPTER 6   **THE ROAD TO GLORY**

THE ARGUMENTS BEGIN
THE ANGER MOUNTS
THE CRITICAL MOMENT
FALLING APART
A FARCICAL GAME
AN UNSTOPPABLE TEAM
THE STRUTTING BEGINS
MOVING UP A GEAR
A LIVERPOOL LIKENESS
THE CONFIDENCE GROWS

6   THE ROAD TO GLORY

Destiny had already allowed itself a few nods in the direction of Liverpool.

The paths of Liverpool and Rafa Benítez seemed destined to cross at some point in the future. They had already encountered each other at decisive moments, though their major encounter would not be for some time to come.

Rafa Benítez led Valencia for the first time at the prestigious Amsterdam tournament in the summer of 2001. His first opponents were to be Liverpool. The match was close, although Liverpool, who had won the UEFA Cup Final a couple of months earlier, were eventually triumphant with a goal by Litmanen. The match was watched on television by thousands of Valencia supporters anxious to see Benítez's debut against a rival of recognised standing. Despite the defeat, their impression was hopeful. Valencia played well in an evenly-matched game. The other teams in the competition were Ajax and AC Milan, who Valencia had beaten during the second leg by 2-1. It was Benítez's first victory with the club from Mestalla – strangely against the team that he most admired.

The rematch with Liverpool came a year later. This time it was on the first day of the 2002-03 Champions League – Benítez's debut in the competition. Valencia won a clear victory on a stiflingly hot night, with a final score of 2-0, and a splendid goal by Pablo Aimar after a magnificently crafted move.

Liverpool, managed by Gérard Houllier, didn't play well and were eventually knocked out after the first round of the tournament. Valencia also won the away leg, through a goal by Rufete. It was the first time that Benítez had set foot in the sanctuary of Anfield and experienced its magic in person.

There was to be yet a fourth confrontation between the two teams. Valencia returned to Anfield in August, 2003 for a friendly. This clash was more significant than anticipated. At that time Benítez was going through a fierce confrontation with Jesús García Pitarch, the sports director of Valencia, over the policy on new signings. The differences between them were well known and had been aired in public. Neither held back and the exchange of accusations made the front pages. The media kept a close watch on a daily basis that summer.

Officials from Valencia used the Liverpool trip to try to calm the troubled waters. The chairman, Jaume Ortí, mediated the conflict and did everything he could to reconcile the two. In time the atmosphere became more relaxed. They began to talk and to explain their positions. The image of Benítez and García Pitarch together on the tiny bench at Anfield seemed to reduce the tension in the air. The best thing, however, was the final result – a 2-0 victory for Valencia with a great goal by Vicente and important saves by Palop. The Liverpool fans, a week from the start of the English league, were quite happy to applaud the stunning performance of the goalkeeper and vote him "man of the match".

The paths of Liverpool and Rafa Benítez seemed destined to cross.

That sunny evening by the Mersey opened a window of opportunity for a promising season. Benítez's team showed signs of some very promising play. It was the first indication of what was to come. The team was still being built, but things were already looking positive. The manager could sense it too. Despite the lack of signings and problems that might arise in the future, Valencia gave off an unmistakable air of a contender with potential. Benítez kept his thoughts to himself, though in some of his comments he couldn't hide his optimism. Some days later, when the squad were officially presented, the manager addressed the thousands of fans who had gathered on the terraces and conveyed a message of optimism.

"The team is working well and I'm getting good vibes. We can achieve important goals, I'm excited."

Benítez's comments brought a hopeful note to an event otherwise marred by anger. The fans repeatedly jeered the Valencia chairman and stopped him reading his planned speech. Popular indignation, resulting from the lack of signings, spoilt the lavish presentation ceremony for Valencia. The public applauded Benítez but showed no respect towards Jaume Ortí. It was a painful night for the chairman. The experience also caused distress to Benítez, who felt sorry for him. It was an unpleasant episode which cooled the spirits of many, and even overshadowed the team's important victory at Liverpool.

The message from the manager was conciliatory, but it wouldn't calm the rage of the supporters towards the chairman and his fellow board members. There were all the signs of a storm brewing, and so it would have been best for the chairman not to speak. But Ortí felt he had to do his job and took on the challenge even though it didn't turn out well. He hadn't wanted to be seen as a coward and so he had decided to face the music.

THE ARGUMENTS BEGIN

Benítez was the favourite of the terraces and there were no protests about him. What was more the fans echoed all his demands and backed the calls to strengthen the team with established players.

The arrival of the Brazilian, Ricardo Oliveira, and the Uruguayan, Canobbio, wasn't enough to satisfy the manager's requests, or the expectations of the fans who were becoming disillusioned.

"I've asked for a table and they've brought me a lamp," Benítez said with obvious annoyance at the pre-season training camp in Switzerland.

This was the tempestuous prelude to the best season in the history of Valencia. No-one dreamt at that turbulent presentation what the outcome would be. It was a rough night which did at least alert the members of the board, the coaches and players to the feelings of their most ardent fans. Everyone got the message and realised their responsibilities.

It was David Beckham's debut in Spain.

The good work that had been done was confirmed in the Trofeo Naranja (Orange Trophy) match against Real Madrid. It was David Beckham's debut in Spain, Madrid's latest acquisition, and it was a summer full of intense media interest in the English star.

There were no goals but Valencia hit the post three times and gave the impression of being better in every department than the team managed by Carlos Queiroz. An improvement on what would occur in the official season. Despite a slip up – a draw at home with Valladolid – in their first outing, Valencia moved into top gear and by the sixth match they were top of the league, with five consecutive victories, having scored in all the games and conceded only one goal.

They had already beaten Madrid and Barça and, apart from the results themselves, had confirmed all of their excellent promise. All the underlying currents which had troubled the organisation in the summer had ebbed away. The waters were calm. Up until the last minute, Benítez had been hoping for the arrival of the Cameroonian, Samuel Eto'o, but the move entailed the departure of the defender Ayala to the ranks of Real Madrid. The deal didn't come off in the end and, after a whole string of rumours and denials, the Argentinian central defender stayed at Mestalla.

Benítez had no doubts about how his team would respond even when their first defeat came against Deportivo – or when their first shock home defeat came against Racing Santander. Valencia kept their spirits up and continued their battle with Real Madrid for top place. After the Christmas truce, the contest hotted up until the end of the first half of the season when Valencia were able to proclaim themselves 'winter champions' after beating Albacete, thanks to a dubious penalty, while the Bernabéu side lost for yet another year in San Sebastián.

Valencia hadn't been in this position halfway through the season since 1947 and this time they had beaten their all time points record. With this mood of euphoria 2004 began, but again a setback lurked on the horizon.

"We need reinforcements, now is the time to improve. The team has done well, but if we want to last out until the end we must have signings in some positions that are shaky."

In principle it was logical and well founded. As the days passed tension grew. The winter transfer window opened and the club had the chance to fill some of the gaps, just as the manager had requested in the summer. The names of several Italian wingers came up – a lot of names – hypothetical suggestions which didn't come off. Everything stayed as it was. No signings.

Benítez exploded. His indignation was obvious at the end of the game against Osasuna at Mestalla. The Navarre side won, thanks to an own goal by

Pellegrino. The press conference was stormy. Unexpectedly, the manager made a drastic declaration:

"I've heard a member of the board who says that we don't need any signings, that the players aren't tired, aren't stale, we'll get as far as we can with what we've got."

That wouldn't be the end of the matter. Warfare broke out again between the coach, the sports director and the board. A three-way battle that also affected the squad. Within a week, Valencia supporters witnessed with astonishment the change in the weather: the sun had gone in, and now storm clouds were gathering which would bring torrential rain.

THE ANGER MOUNTS

When Rafa Benítez gave free rein to his indignation the team were still in three competitions. Their performance had been at a very high level but Benítez was looking beyond that, he was calculating the risks of maintaining such an intense work rate and could foresee problems in the mid-term. He was convinced of the need to make a couple of signings, to help guarantee that they would win the title. For this reason he became less optimistic when assessing objectives.

"Our duty is to be in the top four and qualify for the Champions League. If, once we qualify, we can get further, we'll aim for whatever we can."

He was washing his hands of it and passing responsibility back to the club management. Faced with the umpteenth failure at reinforcing the team, he was stunned into silence. The members of the board ignored his comments and refused to take part in what would be a sterile debate. They had bitter memories of what had happened on the day of the pre-season team presentation.

Benítez knew that he would have to make do with what he had until the end of the season. With some trepidation he accepted the reality, deciding to use his own ingenuity to overcome the challenge. He would have to squeeze everything he could out of the squad. Get one hundred per cent productivity from each and every one of them. He would turn up the heat on the pressure cooker but regulate it skilfully so that it didn't explode before time.

This decision would lead to the players having exceptional demands placed on them and would result in a deterioration of the relationship between the coaching staff and the players. But there was no other solution.

Valencia got back on track with two convincing victories. The first was at Malaga, the lucky charm ground for Benítez, the one of his first League win. There, at La Rosaleda, all doubts disappeared with a crushing victory. Half a dozen goals are a weighty argument in recovering one's optimism. Three of the goals were chalked up by the Brazilian Oliveira in his second hat trick that season – though at home at Mestalla he could only score once in the

Benítez exploded. His indignation was obvious.

whole season. It was as if he got a better view of goal when he played away.

The only setback that evening was when the defender Pellegrino fainted in the first half. The pictures were shocking. He couldn't stand and just slumped to the ground. A major scare. Fortunately, the medical examination afterwards ruled out any serious causes. To play safe though, he was rested for several days. The team had rebuilt its morale, backed by such a spectacular scoreline. They confirmed their excellent form in a comfortable win against Atlético Madrid at Mestalla.

Now the most long-awaited fixture of the season had arrived, the trip to the Bernabéu. A chance to storm the leadership and to seek revenge for being knocked out of the Cup.

The two best teams would face each other.

THE CRITICAL MOMENT

"We have to put in twice as much as we want to get out."

These words would be heard more than once at the Bernabéu from the lips of Rafa Benítez. That February night he reiterated the phrase, an acrimonious expression in the midst of great expectation. Again, the Real Madrid-Valencia game was to end in enormous controversy.

Once again it was Valencia who came off worse. It was the game that would decide the championship – the two main contenders face to face, the two most recent champions in the fray. The atmosphere was strained. It was the first division debut of the referee and, though he wasn't young, he was inexperienced at this level. A dubious penalty was awarded to the home-side in the very last minute. One that was to change the score and the outcome.

Ayala scored, and so Valencia drew a match that they should have won. For days it was the only topic of conversation. The controversy spread. A new incident to feed the fierce rivalry between the two clubs.

For Benítez this was, once again, his jinxed game. It was almost a tradition. It was the highlight of the league, the most watched and most repeated; the media repercussions were staggering. Benítez and his Real Madrid colleague Carlos Queiroz confronted each other. In the press room the Portuguese manager questioned his opponent's style of play. An unpleasant strategy.

The Valencia spirit was seriously undermined. Everything seemed to be going against them. It was the worst moment in the season. Even Benítez seemed to give in. It was as if he had no desire to continue the fight. Everything seemed to be conspiring against him when he needed all the help he could get. He had had his fingers burnt with an ignored request for new players and for standing up to the club's board. Now the ill-fated penalty brought another drubbing. Benítez could see how his team weren't being strengthened despite his insistence and how, for the umpteenth time, he had come away with less than he had hoped for at Real Madrid's ground.

FALLING APART

The scandalous result of their visit to the Bernabéu, and the subsequent rumpus it caused, unsettled Valencia. As had happened two years earlier they again seemed to have lost their way. There was anger and impotence, and this was partly to blame for them only getting a single point, and that from the draw at Madrid, in their next three outings. Immediately after the Madrid game there were two consecutive defeats. Valencia weren't the same. Rafa Benítez knew the dangers that a storm like this could cause, he had already been through them. It wasn't just the game and the Championship which were slipping away to their closest rivals. Now, after what had happened at the Bernabéu, the spotlight was on them. The backlash would be even worse.

Despite all the advice and all the warnings that Benítez impressed on his players in the course of a typical week, he could not prevent his team from falling apart at the seams. There was an intense barrage of statements between Valencia and Madrid. Spanish International players from both Madrid and Valencia were together at the training camp of the national team, preparing for an insignificant friendly against Peru in Barcelona. They were caught in the middle. Marchena and Raúl had both been involved in the Madrid incident. They clashed, along with other players from the two squads. And the press constantly bombarded them with questions about the repercussions of the incident. The importance of the national team was relegated. The timing of this international fixture was extremely bad, not dissimilar to the one that the League fixture list was to throw up.

Valencia were to welcome Barça who were on an upward curve. Benítez had only a couple of days to prepare for the match with his full team. The manager wanted to end the squad's indignation with the refereeing fraternity. But his efforts were in vain. The maelstrom devoured his team. The fans were still furious. Their interest in the game focused on demanding penalties and sending-offs for the slightest reason.

Usually this game is a classic – a sensational and appealing match. Now it turned into an unspectacular contest and one with a strange atmosphere. This didn't stop Barcelona playing well and they won the match with a single move at a point when it had seemed it would end as a 0-0 draw. Benítez demanded concentration but his players seemed on the verge of a nervous breakdown, reckless in their actions and consumed by anxiety as they tried to recover their form. The fans were also adding to the chaos. A good example was when Carboni was sent off in the last moment of the game for hurriedly taking a free kick after the referee had asked another player to move the wall back. The decision was fair, one that could not be disputed. The fans did not agree.

For the team it was a bombshell which unnerved them, particularly as they were well aware that Madrid were winning easily that night at Espanyol's ground and were therefore consolidating their position in first place. The fierce intensity of the row that had been sparked between Real Madrid and Valencia now began to reduce, with the final scores that day helping to cool the spirit of the fans. Valencia's supporters had spent days shouting themselves hoarse in a sterile protest. Madrid fans, on the other hand, pointed to the scoreboard and the absence of favours from the referee as conclusive evidence of their superiority. Valencia had been seriously damaged. It was a blow that hit them hard. Benítez, aware of the his team's demise, began his search for solutions to this emergency. But this was not a team capable of recovering quickly from a situation such as this. Queiroz's team, on the other hand, had come out stronger, watching the resultant chaos from a safe distance – something which suited them.

A week later the crisis deepened. Psychological work had intensified at the Paterna training ground. Benítez wanted to lift his men's spirits. It was essential to get over the trauma that was affecting them and avoid the spread of their downheartedness. Valencia were travelling next to Espanyol, a team whose home record left a lot to be desired. It seemed an excellent opportunity to restore normality.

A FARCICAL GAME

Fate, however, had a surprise in store – snow – an unexpected guest which turned up at the start of the match. A heavy snowfall turned the pitch at the Olímpico stadium into a sea of white in which Valencia ran aground. It was impossible to play football but they played. The referee changed the white ball to an orange one but immediately changed his mind when he realised that Valencia's strip was the same colour. They went back to the original ball despite the snow and the fact the Espanyol's kit was partly white as were their socks. The theatre of the grotesque continued. The game was a sham.

Once again Montjuic was a key setting in the unfolding of events. Just as it had been a couple of years earlier when, on a freezing night, also after a snowstorm, history had taken an unexpected turn. Then Benítez, on the verge of dismissal, had begun an unstoppable march which would lead to the conquest of the League. It had been a memorable recovery.

It was as if Benítez owed a debt from that day, one that destiny hadn't forgotten and would demand payment for at the very worst moment. The Valencia bench were resigned to the spectacle. Benítez didn't even try to get the game suspended when it was clear that in those conditions his team were going under. Nobody reacted or asked the referee to consider postponing the clash. Espanyol were the better side and won. They did so by the narrowest of margins but deservedly so. Deeply depressed, Benítez went to his press conference. His words gave off an air of fatalism. There were no excuses, just acceptance of the reality that in a period of scarcely three weeks Valencia had lost their chance of winning the League. It was as if they were waiting for sentence to be passed – even the elements were against them. No-one felt like talking or giving explanations.

That afternoon, while the squad were returning to Valencia by coach, I spoke to Benítez by mobile phone. I didn't think he would answer the call but he talked far more about events than I had expected. His emotional state was composed. He was thinking of Turkey.

"If the ground had been alright..."

A comment that raised my curiosity: "Rafa, why didn't you ask for a postponement if it looked like you were going to lose?"

His reply was brief.

"The referee wouldn't have agreed and besides we didn't have too many days available for a replay. Now we have to play in Istanbul. But the truth is that nobody raised the issue..."

It was as if at that moment he realised that he had missed a way of stopping the freefall they were in. That day his reflexes had failed him. Valencia were accepting their fate without putting up the slightest resistance. They hadn't been able to look after their interests and had lowered their guard. No attempt was being made to find a logical answer to a situation that was damaging them.

That day his reflexes had failed him.

That passiveness showed the mood of the club and affected every level. It looked like the end of the road. While the squad continued on their return journey, Madrid were winning at home against Celta Vigo without too much effort. A result which was to confirm their supremacy. They now had a comfortable eight point lead. In scarcely two weeks there had been a spectacular turnaround. Valencia had dropped from a position where they could win the title to one a long way from it.

The options seemed to be exhausted.

But the last word was still to be said.

AN UNSTOPPABLE TEAM

Valencia emerged from their black hole. That first Saturday in March they started to move on an upward trajectory.

"The League is still possible."

That was Benítez's message to a small group of journalists gathered for an impromptu midnight meeting at the Mestalla premises. There were no microphones. No-one took any notes. The manager had conducted his press conference with no assumptions about the future, nor had there been any smugness. He was now spilling the beans in an informal meeting.

You could tell that he had got his confidence and his spirits back. He looked different. He exuded confidence, as if he knew the worst was over and that the future would bring great satisfaction. He didn't want to count his chickens but something was stirring, something which allowed him to see the light at the end of the tunnel.

Valencia had beaten Deportivo 3-0 that night, in a match which was much tougher than the scoreline suggested. The Galicians had lost one of their key players, Maura Silva, sent off very early in the game. Earlier Valencia had missed a penalty. There was panic both on the pitch and on the terraces. Then immediately there was a second penalty. Vicente, the Valencian left footer, came forward and scored authoritavely – at last! The Galician team fought bravely until the last moments when Valencia scored two goals. That night Deportivo waved goodbye to their title challenge.

That wasn't the only good news that the Valencia supporters received that day. Real Madrid had drawn at Santander against Racing and, as a bonus, Ronaldo had suffered an injury which was going to keep him out of action for several weeks. That combination of events opened the door to a degree of optimism.

THE STRUTTING BEGINS

The sixth of March was a turning point. From that day on the tables were turned. Valencia began a meteoric rise with six crushing wins in a row. Convincing football, overwhelming scorelines and a clear sense of ambition distinguished Benítez's team. Any doubts about their potential were dispelled. Spurred on by the gap in the table which was narrowing each week, Valencia devoured their opponents while Real Madrid floundered and lost ground. Their lead was getting smaller. Over three weeks Madrid managed to chalk up only two points, Valencia were now just one point from the leaders.

In addition to that, the vibes being given off by the two teams were very different. Valencia were strutting around insolently, Madrid seemed to be almost limping. Again the Montjuic stadium appeared on the horizon. Once again, in the final of the Spanish FA Cup, the Barcelona Olympic mountain seemed to exert a clear influence

On this occasion Benítez was watching the match at home. It was the height of the fiesta of *las fallas* – the eve of the Nit del Foc – when, throughout the city of Valencia, sculptures bearing satirical messages are set light to and burned. It seemed a real allegory.

Benítez wasn't too concened about the result because he believed that everything would depend on his men, but it was an excellent opportunity to check out the form of his main rivals. In the end Zaragoza beat Real Madrid in a fiercely fought final which went into extra time. It was a memorable performance by them.

The blow that the Bernabéu club suffered was to damage their League performance and, later, their Champions League performance. Monaco managed to knock out a club which only a month before had aspired to win the treble. Now Madrid were watching two titles slip away, and they were in serious trouble in the fight for the only one left to win.

Benítez and his team were confident with the idea that Madrid would be knocked out of the title race. "They're not going to hold up, they're going to run out of gas," was a comment that could be heard by those closest to the manager. Benítez had the advantage of privileged information from the capital. From the heart of the club and amongst its entourage he was hearing

Rafa Benítez talks to a group of schoolchildren during his time at Valencia.

stories from friends and from other journalists who knew what was going on. Over and over they repeated the same things. The anarchy of their game and the relaxed training sessions would, sooner or later, take their toll. Time would prove him right.

Madrid lost their next five games – something that had not happened before.

MOVING UP A GEAR

Valencia had conscientiously paced their preparation to come into the final straight of the season with enough resources and with reserves of energy. The hard work carried out by Paco Ayestarán at Paterna bore fruit when they most needed to move up a gear. The Valencia players had great speed and this set them apart. The strength of the players was also much envied.

The reasons for their excellent physical fitness were questioned by some, and unfounded rumours spread. The slander didn't last though. The freshness of their game at this decisive moment allowed them to leapfrog their rivals, and their superiority was clear. In a fairytale second half against Majorca, for example, they scored four of their five goals that evening, with three from Mista, much to the delight of the fans. For a quarter of an hour Valencia played their best football of the season, near perfection. They demolished their opponents. The Majorca manager, Luis Aragonés, the most experienced coach in the League, was unstinting in his praise for his former team.

Valencia were an implacable steamroller. They were like boxers who pinned their opponents to the rope and wouldn't stop until they had annihilated them. The tremendous intensity of their play earned them the nickname of 'The Crushing Machine' with some of the media.

Let them score the goal and leave us alone once and for all!

Benítez had always been irritated by the simplifications of some of the commentators who had described his team as ultra-defensive or of the Italian persuasion, a disparaging cliché which didn't match the reality borne out by the statistics. Their goal difference gave the lie to the descriptions they had branded Valencia with. And now, at last, they were beginning to experience a positive change in the way that they were viewed. In the end their goalscoring rate was comparable to that of the 'galacticos' of Real Madrid and by the end of the season they were the second-highest scoring team, only one goal behind the team from the Bernabéu.

A story that describes the crushing style of their play comes from the match at the Sánchez Pizjuán stadium when they won the Championship with two weeks to spare. Pablo Alfaro, the nimble central defender who played for Sevilla, was overwhelmed by the intensity of their attacks.

"What a pain in the neck they are, let them score the goal and leave us alone once and for all!" he exclaimed.

Before winning at Sevilla they had already won away games in Santander,

Vigo and Saragossa. They, and their fans, had the feeling that the title was close. The night when Valencia went back to the top of the table coincided with Madrid having been spectacularly defeated at home by Osasuna.

A LIVERPOOL LIKENESS

Valencia showed enormous fortitude. They had a style of their own though comparisons were being sought in the spring of 2004. In an informal chat, Benítez admitted what some observers had already commented on publicly: his side's great similarity to that crushing Liverpool team of the late 1970s and early 1980s – a side which dominated Europe with authority, through its power and its balance as a group, rather than through the brilliance of individual players.

Benítez admitted his side's similarity to the Liverpool team of the late 1970s.

Kevin Keegan was to leave after Liverpool's first European Cup win, to be replaced by Kenny Dalglish; two excellent players, but the team excelled because of its collective responsibility. It was a side which swallowed up its opponents, left nothing to chance and had no weak points. The apparent simplicity of their game unnerved their opponents, and they could withstand a physical battle without falling apart. Hostile venues didn't affect them and with the support of their fans at Anfield they were capable of overcoming any side. When they put their foot on the gas nobody could beat them. All the pieces were important; Phil Neal, the right full-back could score, as could the elegant central defender Alan Hansen. In midfield they worked enthusiastically, Souness, McDermott and company, and the men up front took part in every move as well as contributing goals, the lanky Ian Rush, and before him Steve Heighway, and so on.

Benítez's multi-faceted Valencia were similar, with a solidarity which relied on no one individual. A team in which a player such as Pellegrino could, with a well-aimed header, transform a game against a relegation candidate which had become unexpectedly difficult to break down. Someone would always turn it on at the right moment: Rufete at Balaídos, Angulo at Saragossa, Ayala at the Bernabéu or Vicente at El Sardinero. They were all dangerous. Nobody had a monopoly on effectiveness. They worked for the team. That was their great secret, their spirit, they all pulled in the same direction, they were capable of holding back or of taking centre stage and overwhelming opponents who already feared them. That psychological superiority was something they made full use of. No quarter was given. Valencia enjoyed that dominating role but they also knew how to withstand attacks. Getting to that threshold wasn't

No public comment was made, their indignation was held back.

a question of luck, nothing was left to chance. This was the fruit of systematic work, meticulous planning and the commitment of all the players, with the hunger for glory – the mentality of champions.

The final stage of the Championship wasn't free from controversy. Although to judge from the results it was short-lived. The angry exchanges between Valencia and Madrid intensified when Figo was allowed to play at Riazor after having been sent off against Barça following an incident in which Puyol had been injured.

Benítez had no doubt that getting involved in a tit for tat would do no good; he had learnt from previous bitter experience. One of the points now made very strongly in the dressing room was to steer clear of verbal warfare. It had proved fruitless in the past. No public comment was made, their indignation was held back. Only Carboni said something, and then it was with a smile on his lips as if to say that the players couldn't care less about the decisions of football disciplinary committees:

"Everything's fine, we are the best."

Lesson learnt. They weren't going to lose concentration when the title was in sight. Nobody wanted to fall into that trap. Weeks earlier Valencia had already suffered a major upset in the game against Real Sociedad at Mestalla after some poor refereeing. The San Sebastián side were winning 2-0 half an hour from the end and the terraces were up in arms. The Valencia fans were angry, particularly as the day before the Madrid derby at Calderón had gone in favour of Real, thanks to an offside goal scored after a foul on the Atlético goalkeeper.

This anger now transformed into positive energy; the team began to play courageously and saved the match in an epic way, in the last minute, and much to the delight of their fans. The draw, now seemed as good as a victory to Benítez and his players who, affected by the enormous nervous tension they had gone through, were in a state of turmoil. After cooling down a little, they talked in the dressing room about how the refereeing had affected them. They were stunned but preferred to forget it, even though they harboured serious doubts about the fairness of the match that afternoon.

Benítez promptly dispatched the topic at a press conference:

"Of the refereeing I'll say just one thing: it's been very strange."

Matter closed.

The players didn't speak at length on the matter either and were discrete in their comments. There were no explosive outbursts. They played the matter down – though deep down they were still angry.

THE CONFIDENCE GROWS

The qualities they were showing on the pitch were that of a team which didn't give up when faced with a setback. They fought until they dropped. Now they knew which path to take.

It was the last major stumbling block; after that match everything seemed to be on track. Benítez's confidence in his men enabled him to take decisions that the public would accept even though they might not agree with them. At Bilbao, Valencia took to the pitch without their best players in the line-up – held back by the manager. Minutes before the start of the game at San Mamés, Madrid had lost at home to Barça. It was now Valencia's great opportunity to decide the league. Benítez didn't flinch. The resulting draw against Athletic was seen by some as a lost opportunity to put some distance between them and the others. Benítez, on the other hand, stuck to his approach and was happy with the point they won. A week later, another step forward. Madrid lost at La Coruña. They were unlucky, they hit the post three times, but their opponents unnerved them and they fell apart. They lost 2-0 with Zidane being sent off before half-time.

"Rafa, have you been watching the match?"

"Yes I watched it for a while, but now I'm playing with my daughter."

"I don't believe it, you've stopped watching?"

"What's important now is what we do tomorrow, if we carry on in the same way it doesn't matter what Madrid do."

This conversation took place at half-time. Rafa was relaxed, assured and calm. He had already made his announcement to the journalists that morning:

"It's up to us now, if we win our remaining matches we'll be the Champions."

It was the first time he had stated in public a possibility which, up till then, he had avoided talking about.

Benítez learnt of the final result while he was at home. He didn't experience it with the intensity you would have expected or with the passion that the Valencia supporters celebrated their own victory the next day against Betis. A clear, well deserved win, with no stridency or suffering. Everything went to plan.

Yes I watched it for a while, but now I'm playing with my daughter.

The great week had now arrived when Valencia would conquer the League and reach the UEFA Cup Final. For this reason their game against Sevilla in the league had to be played on Sunday. Madrid and Barcelona who were in the middle of miraculous recoveries, had to play a day earlier on the Saturday, because of television schedules. Madrid weren't happy with this because they felt that Valencia would have the advantage of knowing the results of their competitors. But there was no flexibility, those who held the television rights to the League were in control and they had to fit in with their plans.

Both teams lost. Barça in Vigo against Celta who fought agonisingly hard to stay up; Madrid, at home against a superior Majorca side. Both defeats would serve up the title on a plate for Valencia if they could win against

Sevilla in their away match.

That Saturday night, just as the week before, Benítez didn't pay too much attention to the screen. If he had he would have witnessed the sinking of the Madrid Titanic with Samuel Eto'o in the starring role. Benítez sat calmly in the bar of the hotel, with his back to the set, while the Valencia supporters prepared for a last minute pilgrimage to Seville so as not to miss the chance to sound their second victory chant in three seasons. He had no doubts: Valencia wouldn't fail.

He had hardly had a day's rest after the demanding confrontation with Villarreal in the semi-finals of the UEFA Cup but the momentum of the team could overcome any obstacle. Before heading to the stadium, in the solitude of his room, Rafa Benítez received a visit from some friends. They had gone down at the last minute to be at the match. He was serene, much more relaxed than his excited visitors, who were disconcerted by his calmness.

"I've got the team more or less sorted out, I've just got one problem to find an answer to but it's nothing too important."

He wouldn't give any more clues. He didn't give any names but in the line-up some heavyweights were missing and two of the reserves, Xisco and Sissoko, appeared. It didn't matter. It took less than 10 minutes. Vicente scored. In the streets of Valencia they began to celebrate. It was a special day and by a strange coincidence it was also the day of Valencia's Patron Saint: Virgen de los Desamparados. In the final minutes of the game Baraja scored the second goal – it was all over. The Seville fans accepted defeat gracefully and sportingly congratulated the new champions.

Benítez, a man in whom few had put any trust at the beginning, had given Valencia its sixth League Championship. And there were still two weeks left of the League season.

When the manager appeared it was to the expected script: controlled joy, acknowledgements and personal dedications – and a trace of feigned resentment. He had more than surpassed his target but exhaustion had taken its toll on him.

The next day thousands awaited the return of the champions. The whole city turned out. The images from two years earlier were repeated, but this time there was no rain and the sun shone. It was an unforgettable party from the moment the plane touched down mid-afternoon at Manises. The Valencia captain, Albelda, could be seen in the pilot's cabin leaning out over the tarmac and waving a *senyera*, the flag of the Valencia region. This would be one of the first memorable pictures of a day full of emotion.

Benítez stayed in the background, handing over to his players who enjoyed themselves like children. His job was done. The result was unsurpassable.

Rafa BENÍTEZ

>> CHAPTER 7 **GOODBYE VALENCIA**

A FATEFUL SUBSTITUTION
AN EXTRAORDINARY DEFEAT
THIRD TIME LUCKY
ROTATION
HARD TIMES AND A HAPPY ENDING
RETURN TO TURKEY
GOODBYE VALENCIA
THE BOMBSHELL HITS
STORM CLOUDS

7   GOODBYE VALENCIA

The Cup competition was a cross which Benítez had to bear in his three seasons at Valencia.

In his first two seasons, there were two bizarre eliminations from the Spanish FA Cup. The first for fielding an improper line-up, the other in a penalty shoot-out after extra time despite having led by two goals. Both matches were against second division B teams. His last involvement in the competition was critical and had an impact on the team. Real Madrid had knocked them out with a comprehensive scoreline that didn't reflect what had happened on the pitch.

What is certain is that Benítez, and by extension his men, choked on this tournament. It was as if a curse were following him. It seemed as though there would be unexpected surprises each time – that he just wasn't destined to succeed. No matter how much he tried he could never reach the semi-finals.

In Spain the system used is one of single match knockouts with games being played on the lower division side's home ground. Benítez was never convinced by it, and was one of a number of prominent managers who were unhappy with the terms of the competition.

With his move to England and Liverpool FC he was to take part in the mother of all cup competitions: the FA Cup, the oldest football tournament in the world. Whilst Benítez found the system fairer it didn't go much better for him in this competition either, and Liverpool found themselves knocked out at an early stage by Burnley.

And so it began to seem almost as if Rafa Benítez was a manager whose character wasn't suited to cup competition. A League campaign demands a more rational approach to planning. In any cup competition spur of the moment inspiration and spark prevail; there's little chance to change things – though, of course, it's very thrilling when matches go to the wire. But Benítez doesn't like to take risks, nor does he seem comfortable when he has to.

And then, of course, along came Liverpool's spectacular Champions League campaign of 2004-05.

A FATEFUL SUBSTITUTION

Benítez's most calamitous setback with Valencia happened at Novelda. It was scarcely a month and a half into the 2001-02 season – the first round in the Cup against a second division B team. Conditions are almost always the same in this type of confrontation; the big teams feel out of place in the ground, whilst their opponents are spurred on by the enthusiastic fans packing the tiny grounds. At least on this occasion the pitch was in impeccable condition.

Benítez had taken the match seriously, he didn't want any upsets, he hadn't been long in the job and needed to gain credibility. He had conscientiously studied videos of his opponents and the majority of his first-team players were in the line-up.

It was a hard fought game but there were very few chances and the first-half ended 0-0. In the second, Valencia began to take charge. It wasn't an overwhelming supremacy but you could see the difference in class. The goal for Valencia, the work of Rufete, came from an isolated piece of play. From that moment on Novelda played desperately for a draw and the team from Mestalla sought to take advantage. The last few minutes were exhausting and Benítez decided to use his three substitutes to cool the contest down and break the

It seemed almost as if Rafa Benítez was a manager not suited to cup competition.

rhythm of the local team. The last substitution was to prove fateful.

Vicente came off and was replaced by the Romanian Dennis Serban. For the last few minutes Valencia were playing with a non-European player in excess of the number permitted under Spanish FA rules. Initially nobody noticed until, up in the VIP box, Jesús Barrachina, a member of the Valencia board, realised the illegal manoeuvre. Too late. The game ended in victory for the visitors by 1-0, but the win was worthless.

News raced round the corridors of the La Magdalena stadium, though it was not until they were on the coach home that some Valencia players discovered the blunder. Benítez appeared annoyed in the post-match press conference. He took responsibility for what had happened and said that he was dismayed. The tension of the match had distracted him from realising the tremendous mistake he had made. That night he could hardly sleep. It was a huge disappointment. He relived that wretched substitution with me: all the details, one by one, to understand the causes. One player, anxious to get on the pitch, to have an opportunity to show his qualities; another coming off, exhausted and released from stress; fellow players holding on to a narrow lead. The fact that, despite the attempts of the club, the Argentinian Ayala had not been accepted as a European player also had a bearing on the incident.

Nor was there anyone on the bench to warn him, not even the assistant

That night he could hardly sleep. It was a huge disappointment.

coach, Antonio López, nor the team delegate, Juan Cruz Sol, a distinguished former Valencia and Real Madrid international. This fact would cost Sol his job because it had not been the first time he'd made the mistake. He'd already been involved in an identical situation, albeit in a league game that Valencia had lost at Santander, though then the mistake hadn't had the same consequences, as they'd lost the match anyway. This time not only did it change the result, but the match was also a qualifier with no return leg. The Cup was over for Valencia.

The Spanish Federation declared Novelda winners. Valencia put forward the case that there were no precedents in the Cup competition and stressed the unusual fact that it was a single leg qualifier. It did them no good. Neither did their veiled attempts to get Novelda to drop the matter, something which led to speculation about attempted bribery.

Manolo Maciá replaced Sol, who was desolate to be leaving the club. Later he would return to Mestalla, along with his colleagues from the 1971 League Championship team, to take the honorary kick-off at the last league match won by Benítez's team – an emotional act.

For Valencia it was a tough blow, both at a sporting and at a financial level. Benítez also came out badly from this incident.

When Benítez next took part in the tournament he was affected by the memory of what had happened at the La Magdalena stadium. This painful fiasco was added to two previous failures under the management of Héctor Cúper. The first, when they were knocked out in a penalty shoot-out at the ground of Guadix, one of the poorer sides of second division B, after a crazy game which had ended in a four goal draw; and the other, a two leg game against Osasuna, then a second division side.

Valencia were beginning life as League Champions but were also facing the trauma of this assorted collection of blunders.

When they crossed swords with Nàstic of Tarragona, Benítez's team had had an excellent start in both the Spanish League and the Champions League. But there was very nearly another upset. The Catalan team, with their fans behind them, forced extra time and a penalty shoot-out after a 0-0 draw.

Valencia scored all five and their goalkeeper, Palop, stopped one from the home team, ensuring that Valencia went through to the next round, but it was a close call.

Another single leg draw and once again against a rival from group 3 of second division B: Alicante. They had already eliminated another first division team in the first round: Espanyol. Benítez chose a line-up of players who didn't usually play in League matches – his famous rotation system, putting players considered as reserves into the first-team. That night in the Rico Pérez stadium we witnessed that football can be a capricious and jack-in-the-box sport which, at any given moment, goes beyond logic. Valencia scored first. They weren't playing well but their quality was still superior. Alicante fought back with conviction and managed to equalise. Nothing remarkable, the game progressed in a not unusual way – the heavyweights performed sluggishly and with little motivation, whilst their opponents were full of optimism. Both goals came in the second half and extra time had to be played. The outlook wasn't good for a Valencia side already chastened in the Cup.

Failures had come one after another since their glorious 1999 win, their last title – when they had beaten Barça, who had won the cup in the previous two years, in the quarter-finals; then Real Madrid in the semi-finals, with a spectacular 6-0 win; and Atlético Madrid in the final.

AN EXTRAORDINARY DEFEAT

On that warm night in November 2002 Rafa Benítez may have been aware of the demands which were being placed on the club after their series of absurd experiences. He sensed that his team had fallen into the web of these qualifying rounds which had become a death trap for the bigger Spanish football teams. He played his winning card. He resorted to his big guns. Aimar and Baraja swung into action to set things right in extra time. Events proved

From the first 10 penalties everyone scored – not a single failure.

him right. Valencia scored two goals and the situation seemed under control. Even the Alicante fans had resigned themselves to defeat and had begun to leave the terraces five minutes before the end.

The Alicante players hardly had any strength left after their enormous efforts and seemed to have given up the qualifying round for lost, their greatest concern now seemed to be to swap shirts with their famed rivals. Suddenly the game took an unpredicted turn. A lapse of concentration by the defenders led to a second goal for the home team. That isolated incident breathed new life into Alicante. Another lapse in the Valencia defence led to a corner. Alicante had the last opportunity of the night and took it. A miraculous goal in the final gasp of the match left Valencia like the boxer on the verge of being knocked out. Dazed by the blow, gripped by nerves, Benítez's men had no choice but to face the predicament of a penalty shoot-out.

The spectators who had left the ground hurried back to their places, incredulous at such a recovery. Benítez spoke to his players to prepare them for the kicks. It was not a time for reproaches. The players had hardly absorbed what had happened. They couldn't believe it. Benítez couldn't either, but he had to react. He talked to them coolly and calmly. He asked for volunteers. Those who were sure of themselves came forward. The manager chose the order and encouraged the players, reminding them of the previous qualifying match which they had won through penalties.

The Alicante players had nothing to lose.

They were the ones who had achieved this extraordinary outcome and now faced it resolutely and less nervously. From the first 10 penalties everyone scored – not a single failure. Alicante were to kick first and scored with their sixth. The goalkeeper, Palop, was becoming desperate. Now it was Fabio Aurelio's turn for Valencia. The fans gathered behind the goal cheering on the goalkeeper of the Spanish national team. Their support was effective. The Brazilian struck his shot powerfully but the goalkeeper stopped it – a reflex save. The shock was complete. Jubilant fans invaded the pitch and Valencia went out of the competition through the tradesman's entrance. Benítez tried to find a logical explanation to what had happened but there wasn't one. Determined to find the causes for the debacle, he highlighted the overconfidence of his team, their complacency when everything seemed to be wrapped up. This had been the determining factor.

THIRD TIME LUCKY

A year later Valencia escaped being knocked out prematurely but it led to controversial consequences. They were to meet Castellón. Their opponent's supporters were enthusiastic and the atmosphere tense, remnants of an old rivalry. The local club was managed by professed Valencia supporters: its chairman, Antonio Bonet, was an important shareholder; its sports manager, Fernando Gómez, had worn the Valencia shirt on more occasions than anyone; and their manager, José Luis Oltra, who had coached at Paterna. They were all excitedly looking forward to the confrontation, aware of their chances. Castellón had attracted the attention of Spanish football the previous season when they had smashed the records by going more than 30 matches without defeat. In the final game for promotion they had just missed the boat and hadn't gone up. Now they had won the jackpot in the Cup.

Benítez found himself with a new opportunity to make amends for the fiascos of Novelda and Alicante.

At the time Valencia were League leaders and were playing well. They had beaten Atlético Madrid, Real Madrid and Barcelona in consecutive matches and with great authority. But the planned date was one of those black holes in the fixture list which improvisation and carelessness had managed to allocate just before a Spanish international game.

Here was the first disagreement. Benítez insisted on having his international players and so the match was brought forward by a day. The Federation, conscious of the blunder, authorised the change and allowed the clubs affected to use the players who had been called up for the national team.

Valencia had less than 48 hours rest between the League game they had played at the Nou Camp and their cup match in Castellón, but at least they could call upon their international players. Despite this, only Albelda was in Benítez's first team. Castellón walked all over Valencia in a jubilant first half. They deserved their goals. Benítez had fielded an experimental team, holding back the majority of his key players. In the second half he balanced things out. Castellón began to run out of steam and Valencia, with their best men on the pitch, levelled the match. One of the top reserves, Baraja, equalised with a header and would have changed the balance even further from the penalty spot had it not been for a spectator who assaulted the referee, Téllez Sánchez, by throwing something from the terraces. The temperature was rising when the referee decided to suspend the match. Tension gripped the stadium. A chaotic ending, nerves jangling; a setback for everyone as they awaited the decision of the competition committee.

BEHIND CLOSED DOORS

The decision was to play the match behind closed doors on the same ground. The time remaining to be played was to start with the penalty which had triggered the conflict between the two managers. Both men played the game of psychological warfare, spurred on by the media hype that surrounds this sort of match. The pantomime lasted right up to the very last minute, with Benítez stretching it out as long as he could. In the morning there was a training session behind closed doors at the Paterna sports complex where the players practised penalties.

Baraja seemed to have been the one chosen but there were doubts. The team didn't have a regular penalty taker and much less a reliable one. Since the departure of Mendieta they had missed too many. The other side pulled their rabbit out of the hat – in this case, the goalkeeper. The first team goalkeeper, Oliva, had, against all odds, given up his place to the reserve, Raúl.

At the appointed time this ceremony of confusion reached its high point when the players in the orange strip went up to the penalty spot. They began kicking the ball from one to another. Baraja gave way to Mista and he in turn to Vicente. All day nerves had been on edge, the most trivial detail acquiring the status of privileged information – industrial espionage in favour of the enemy. Television pictures from the training session broadcast at midday had enraged Benítez, even though they didn't reveal anything, and simply confused matters. They didn't even last 30 seconds and all that could be seen was Baraja at the ominous penalty spot, and he wasn't going to take it anyway.

The operetta came to an end when Mista told the referee that he was going to take the kick. Raúl, the goalkeeper, stopped the shot but the ball landed at the feet of Baraja who finally scored. It was like tempting fate. But there was time for a lot more. Castellón were heroic and equalised. Then followed a controversial tackle which looked like a clear penalty for them. The referee didn't blow.

Shortly after, Valencia decided the match with a third goal. In the final minute Benítez made a substitution. To the benches of the home team this was seen as provocation. Jorge Simó, the fitness coach, who had been a colleague of Benítez at university and at Madrid, walked over to the visitors' bench making disapproving gestures. It was the start of hostilities. Angry exchanges began between the two coaches. It reached its peak in the press room after the match. Oltra was upset by what he considered an insult from a colleague. He accused him publicly of disrespect by making an unnecessary substitution when the game had already been decided.

Benítez justified his decision and said that it had been planned beforehand. He rejected any intention of causing offence. Both men then had a bitter confrontation in the corridors of Castalia. There were strong words and mutual accusations. It was the unpleasant epilogue to a qualifier, one which left a nasty taste in the mouth and many open wounds.

"The Cup – as far as we can go," was the slogan the manager repeated to his colleagues in the coaching team. No target was set, but Benítez was hungry for the next match. The match against Castellón had been too exhausting.

These games had become a nightmare, tough obstacles with no positive consequences. Valencia pushed ahead and breathed a sigh of relief. In the end it was a favourable draw, a match against a modest opponent: Murcia, one of the minnows of the first division and the game was to be played as a single leg at Mestalla. It all went according to plan and Valencia won with no complications. The next round was less pleasurable and over two legs. It was against Osasuna and the return match was in Pamplona. Valencia got the game off on the right tracks with two goals but things became difficult. Curro Torres got two yellow cards. A refereeing error led to a disproportionate reaction from the player, and it was right next to the home bench.

Benítez went wild when he saw his attempts at calming the player down had failed. The right winger was to pay for it with a prolonged stay in the reserves, with his punishment beginning three days later in Albacete. At the first opportunity the manager made it clear that he had zero tolerance for this type of attitude. Almost without wanting it, Osasuna found themselves making a comeback and they ended up with a 2-2 draw. Valencia went to El Sadar as 'winter champions' and needed to win. Benítez firmly believed he could but he was concerned about the cost. Absolute concentration and considerable effort were needed against the Navarre team on their home turf. Valencia went into the game fully convinced. They played authoritatively. Two goals, one in each half, put an end to a thrilling contest.

THE OLD ENEMY

Halfway through the season the two top teams in the League, and by now already the only real contenders for the title, had to meet each other in the Cup. Valencia and Madrid were to play for a place in the semi-finals. They were also settling the score as to who was the best team in Spain. That's how the football press presented it in dramatic headlines – the clash of the Titans. The duel would feed the fierce rivalry between both clubs.

For Benítez the trip to the Bernabéu meant that he could measure the potential of his team against his most dangerous rivals, but more than anything he wanted to use it as an opportunity to undermine Madrid. Benítez was convinced of his men's chances. He also knew perfectly well that Real were being increasingly criticised and that many questions were being asked about the disappointing failure of their 'galacticos' stars.

He was so confident that he decided to go all out to win the match. A clear strategy, and with it a specific slogan – "Go get 'em" – just as the fans chant in the grounds when they want to breathe enthusiasm into their teams. And that's how it was that Valencia had Real Madrid against the ropes during the first quarter of an hour and had three clear chances at goal. On the terraces there was a deathly silence in response to Madrid's obvious inferiority. But Benítez couldn't guarantee they would score and that's why the game started to change and why the result turned out as it did.

Whilst Valencia missed chance after chance, without hitting the target, Queiroz's team scored with their only opportunity of the first half. At half-time Benítez insisted, "Don't worry about their goal, the most important thing is that we should score." Again Valencia put the pressure on when the game restarted but they couldn't score. Mista had his worst night of the whole season, missing innumerable chances until his manager took him off.

Little by little Madrid and their fans settled into the game and a second goal came. It looked like being the final goal but as always with these sort of matches there was to be controversy. The referee, Medina Cantalejo, gave a penalty in Madrid's favour after an incident involving Marchena and Raúl. It was a serious refereeing error. A repeat of the most controversial incident of the 2003-04 League and one which, a few weeks later, would lead to the same players being involved in the same situation. It was the third goal and the deciding one.

His excessive ambition had led him to adopt a risky strategy.

That night Benítez learnt a lesson. His excessive ambition had led him to adopt a risky strategy. Yes he had been one step away from demolishing the Bernabéu with the crushing start his team had had. In the end though everything had been reversed. Perhaps in the Cup he could allow himself these excesses, but now it was clear to him that in the next visit to Madrid he would adopt exactly the opposite approach.

Now there were the doubts about the return tie. Was it worth burning up energy and insisting on massive effort for a mission which was unlikely to be successful? The Valencia fans were crying out for revenge. As the game drew closer the ambient temperature rose. More than 40,000 tickets were sold. Benítez had been undecided at first but, eventually, caught up by the fervour of the fans, he left the door open for a miracle. Deep inside he was aware of the enormous challenge of beating Madrid 4-0 or of drawing and forcing extra time. In the League they had won by 2-0. All the fans at Mestalla would be throwing themselves behind the pursuit of an epic victory. There was the memory of the 6-0 defeat suffered by Madrid in 1999 – but this could only distract the team.

Valencia were still challenging in the League and were in the UEFA Cup. The massive effort required could leave the team damaged in many ways. In the end Benítez opted for a compromise approach. Go out hell for leather and go for revenge if things are going well. But if not, he would opt for stopping the team from getting unnecessarily exhausted. Spurred on by their

No player is indispensable, although some are more important than others.

devoted following, Valencia came out at full speed – too fast – more heart than head. Their aggressive approach made them play without any accuracy and they ran around as if possessed. Madrid were calm and orderly, hardly breaking sweat. The *coup de grâce* came very soon. There had scarcely been a quarter of an hour of optimism. Madrid scored and the boiler room at Mestalla shut down. What followed was a mere formality. The terraces accepted with resignation the successive substitutions ordered by the bench – a clear recognition that there was nothing they could do.

Far from getting angry with the manager the fans began to chant his name loudly and insistently and to demand the dismissal of the board of directors. It was an outrageous reaction but one which expressed their collective frustration. Amidst the general disenchantment, Benítez asked for calm. He didn't want to stoke up the controversy despite the lack of support he had received. He was cautious and summed up the tie wisely:

"The aggregate final score is exaggerated. The difference between the two teams in the two games as a whole has not been so great. We lost the tie at the Bernabéu – that penalty ended up sinking us."

A statement of regret that would be repeated and magnified before long.

ROTATION

"No player is indispensable, although some are more important than others."

Rafa Benítez follows this maxim to the letter.

I heard him say this after winning his second League title. He was already thinking about the future and his plans recognised the possibility that even players who were considered 'untouchable' might leave. Some of the key players of that campaign would have had a difficult future if Benítez had stayed in the job. For him no matter how high profile a player was, their continuance at the club was not guaranteed – a very different approach to most managers.

Another of his peculiarities was the continual change to line-ups.

It's very possible that the term 'rotation' will be associated with Rafa Benítez more than with anyone else. He became well-known because of his use of the rotation system, and he also brought the term to public attention. Some discredited his policy from the outset without really giving it proper consideration. For them it was simply frivolous. They also denounced the manager as a 'smart Alec'. The crushing traditional logic – that in football the best men always had to play – was seen as an irrefutable truth. It was seen as the infallible recipe for success. An approach which allowed for no variation.

"You might as well experiment with lemonade," was another clichéd contribution from the critics.

Time and success quietened the dissenting voices. In the end, almost everyone started to accept the wisdom of a work schedule which was proving beneficial. This acceptance began with the players themselves and the 'team' became the most important thing.

Use of the rotation system has become a necessity for a team to be able to face the demands of an increasingly saturated fixture list. At Valencia, during the 2003-04 season, five players were regularly called up for the national side and Ayala and Aimar crossed the Atlantic on many occasions to play for Argentina. A footballer's performance, over the nine months of official competition, becomes less effective as a result of all this travelling. And, of course, in addition to this there are the injuries and minor strains, and the 38 League games and 13 UEFA Cup games that Valencia played before being proclaimed champions, and a further 6 games in the Spanish FA Cup.

Faced with this – as well as the tiring journeys, training camps and other complications – the plans and the preparation for some commitments were subject to a whole host of risks. As time passes and unforeseen events crop up, coaches have to adapt the plans that they have made at the beginning of the season. Benítez, always wishing to control things down to the last detail, was forced to adapt in the face of the reality of events.

Football nowadays is very demanding and players are subject to a greater amount of wear and tear, particularly at the more successful clubs. Squads have come to be more important than the teams. With this maxim, Benítez worked hard to find a way to use all of his players, modifying the line-up week by week. With the exception of the goalkeeper, nobody was excluded from sitting it out on the bench.

The goalkeepers had already been allocated to the competitions in which they were to play: Cañizares for the League, Palop for the Spanish FA Cup and the UEFA Cup.

Events proved Benítez to be right. As his last season at Valencia progressed, the team faced an extremely tough final stretch in excellent form and finished up winning both possible titles. They all did their bit and played their part in this brilliant achievement. In the end the difference between the leading actors and the supporting ones was blurred. A picture best sums up this statement: that of Baraja and Aimar, two of the most sought-after members of the squad, warming up on the sidelines of Sánchez Pizjuán during the second half of the game against Sevilla in which Valencia won the League title. Though it was a decisive match, plans weren't altered nor was the way of thinking modified. Everything went to plan, allowing the fans the opportunity to sing a victory chant even before learning of the defeats of Madrid and Barça. Valencia had fought the return game of the semi finals of the UEFA Cup against Villarreal on the Thursday and the substitutions had been planned. Benítez didn't stray at all from the script, to the amazement of some sceptics who had expected him to field eleven star players. Valencia won with the authority of champions without feeling the absence of some of their top players. His objective was to win the League and he took advantage of the first opportunity to do so.

SUPPORT AT LAST

As time passed Benítez won the approval and support of the Valencia fans. He had gained credibility and, as his period at Mestalla progressed, few dared disagree with his decisions, especially concerning line-ups and substitutions.

But it wasn't always that way. At first he had battled against the incomprehension of the majority of the public and the critics. Amongst journalists bets were taken on match days before the final eleven were confirmed. The guesses were rarely right and some felt that all the week's work, attendance at training sessions at Paterna, personal assumptions and tips from third parties were useless. Predictions would come to nothing. There was always some surprise in the line-up, and the players were the first to be surprised. The manager maintained his custom of announcing the team in the dressing room an hour and a half before the start of the match, after the players had got off the coach.

At first he had battled against the incomprehension of the majority of the public.

Aimar was his greatest problem, as he had been for Cúper. The Argentinian manager had been crucified for not including him in some of the games. Everybody clamoured for Aimar, they all wanted him in the first team. In their songs the fans put him on a pedestal along with the incomparable Mario Kempes and the very fast Claudio Piojo López, all three players from Argentina. Pablo Aimar had particular characteristics that needed gradual adaptation to the rhythm of the Spanish League. Cúper used him sparingly, so too did Benítez. Both were criticised. The directors also jumped on this bandwagon. The decision to sign the young star from River Plate had involved the biggest financial outlay in the history of the club and Valencia's precarious financial situation couldn't afford for this to be wasted. Aimar was a good investment, his value was rising, and he was considered a match winner, capable of influencing the outcome of a game. Javier Subirats, the man who had pushed through the contract of the up-and-coming star and the person who fought most to bring him to Valencia, also complained about the inflexibility of the coaches. Using a collective team system drowned out the indisputable talent of the player born in Río Cuarto.

A tricky question and a difficult one to solve. It wouldn't be the only one.

October 2001, the first week of the League, Alavés were visiting Mestalla. The game was dull – no goals, no chances, just yawns. Valencia needed someone capable of putting the solid defence of the Alavés team, managed by Mané, under pressure.

The fans grew impatient as the second half went on. Everything continued as before. The terraces were clamouring for more strikers to be brought on. Time and time again Valencia crashed against the defensive wall of the

Benítez didn't lose his composure and appeared impassive.

visitors. Benítez didn't lose his composure and appeared impassive as the barrage rained down on him. Twenty minutes from the end he made the substitution that people were calling for, he took off the holding midfielder and put on a striker.

Far from satisfying the crowd their indignation increased. They felt that this substitution, which everyone had known for some time was needed, was too late. Benítez didn't flinch. Aimar, with the inclusion of a new attacker, turned the game upside down but the scoreboard remained unchanged. An explanation was given later. The substitution was pre-planned as it was believed that tiredness would begin to take its toll on the Basque players, who had been determined from the very first minute to prevent Valencia from scoring. Aimar could find more space in this context and capitalise on his strengths.

Benítez's explanation didn't convince many and they didn't hesitate to express their disapproval. If at home, faced with a strong defence, Aimar couldn't count on more backup in attack, how did Benítez intend to win this type of game – risks had to be taken?

That evening he was on a programme broadcast by Canal Nou called *Minut a Minut* and had an interesting conversation with Quique Sánchez Flores. It began in the studio and continued outside in a corridor where, for almost an hour, they put across their points. Benítez was looking for someone to whom he could explain his ideas openly. Quique, at that time a television commentator, was also a budding manager who was finishing his training and was curious to learn of Benítez's ideas in greater detail.

A few weeks later, the story was repeated in a similar fashion. Another team with no great aspirations, Tenerife, ruined the afternoon at Mestalla in a carbon copy of the previous match, another 0-0 draw. There was unrest on the terraces and Benítez was the object of a rude gesture from one of his players of which he was unaware until he saw it a little later on television. He made a substitution, Vicente came on for Kily González. The Argentinian international purposefully avoided the affectionate slap on the back from the manager as he made his way towards the bench. When asked about it, Benítez reacted as best as he could, he didn't attach any great importance to it, but on the inside he was furious. González paid for his lack of respect with some unexpected time on the substitutes' bench.

Benítez remained faithful to his beliefs and outside pressure didn't affect him too much. If anything it inspired him to look for convincing answers to the permanent bombardment he had to put up with every time that the natural substitute for Maradona – according to Diego Maradona himself – didn't come out on to the pitch at the start of a game. The fact was that Aimar was at his best in the final weeks of the season when Valencia moved full steam ahead to comfortably take the League Championship. That's when the great Pablito came to prominence, the idol of the Valencia supporters, with memorable goals that won both matches against Tenerife and Deportivo, and with performances that will go down in history, like the second half against Espanyol at Mestalla. He was unanimously considered the key factor in their success. His freshness was due in part to his specific training plan – daily workouts at training sessions focused on improving his fitness and adapting it to the European rhythm of play. These produced the desired result. Aimar

Paco Ayestarán, the fitness trainer who is now on the Liverpool bench with Rafa Benítez.

arrived at games bursting with energy and his performance matched his reputation. But not everybody agreed with Benítez's strategy. There were those who believed that Aimar should have spent more time on the pitch, arguing that if he had Valencia would have won the title sooner. We'll never know, but Aimar's best form since joining Spanish football was shown in those two and a half months.

Nevertheless, use of the rotation system was not as significant until Benítez's second season at Valencia when they were defending both the League title and in the Champions League. Paco Ayestarán, the fitness trainer, agreed with Benítez that the workload should be shared out if they wanted to guarantee reaching the final third of the competition, the decisive phase, in which those teams who arrive with their energy tanks still full have the greatest chance of winning.

In the first stage of the Champions League it was made quite clear that membership of the first team would be carefully controlled. Valencia were on the verge of achieving an almost complete run of victories, five victories and a draw over six games. The only match in which they didn't achieve three points – played in Basel in front of a lively home crowd – showed very clearly that the performance of the team could be effectively controlled from the bench, to match the importance of the game.

Benítez didn't want to push too much and so he took his foot off the accelerator, using an experimental line-up and giving opportunities to less frequently used players. He was one step away from winning against the surprise team in the group who were to go forward in second place to Valencia. Behind them they would leave by the wayside two illustrious teams – Liverpool and Spartak Moscow.

This, without doubt, was one of the most thought-provoking elements that could be seen in the Valencia team under his management: that of controlling the performance of the players and regulating the intensity of their play.

In some matches it was plain to see. The team would slow down or speed up its rate of play under instruction from the coach, but always in relation to the needs of the fixture list. This strategy was totally contrary to normal practice. Johan Cruyff could, from time to time, deliver a surprise with some unexpected novelty such as the sacrifice of some 'untouchable' player, but his substitutions weren't at the level of a planned philosophy. For Cruyff it was the combination of his particular vision of football and spur of the moment inspiration. Benítez was more calculating and his rotations, always in the plural, were based on a more extensive concept which stretched over the whole season.

HARD TIMES AND A HAPPY ENDING

On Tuesday 11th September 2001, Rafa Benítez and the Valencia squad got ready to set out on a journey to a faraway Caucasian republic. Benítez was to make his debut in European competition against an almost unknown opponent.

In the city of Novorossiysk they would play a club called Chernomorets, his first opponents in the 2001-02 season. Before the draw the manager and the majority of the players had stated their preference:

"We don't care who we get, the only thing we would like, given the choice, is a trip to a nearby country and a comfortable journey."

The season was just beginning, the teams were going through a period of fine-tuning, and they were nowhere near reaching their best form. Valencia were one of the leading clubs in the tournament, the team to beat – they had just come from playing two finals in the Champions League. The result of the draw was far from what Benítez had wanted for his European debut. Luck had dealt him a qualifying round not exactly in the interests of the Mestalla club. His baptism of fire would take him on an almost four-hour flight to a distant region of the former Soviet Union. On paper not a bad draw but in practice there were too many non sports-related drawbacks.

When he heard of the draw he had to look for their opponents on the map. There is another city with an identical name situated in the remote lands of Siberia. General relief. At least this Novorossiysk – a port on the Black Sea near the Sea of Azov, in the Republic of Krasnodar – was a temperate zone, a very popular tourist destination in Russia and close to the Ukrainian city of Odessa.

Valencia took off from the airport at Manises mid-morning on that Tuesday for the little-known destination, ready to fulfil their obligations, without too much enthusiasm for the trip and aware of their clear superiority although knowledge of their adversary was limited. Everything went smoothly, nothing of note during the long flight.

On landing mobile phones were switched back on. Someone raised the alarm. "Something's happened in New York, there's been an attack on the Twin Towers."

Almost all members of the squad had received text messages on their phones. These were moments of confusion and contradictory stories. Some of the group tried to get news by asking the airport staff. They wanted more details. Faced with the harshness of the images confronting them on television, the Valencia party had to resort to their elementary knowledge of English, which some of the locals could speak, to try to understand what was going on. They also used their phones to search for the latest news, to find out any detail they could about the tragedy. The squad huddled around a rudimentary set in a room in the very old terminal building. They began to take in the magnitude of what had happened. They were stunned. Some recalled their trips to the Big Apple and photos that had been taken on the terrace of one of the emblematic Towers which no longer existed.

At that time of emotional impact, deeply distressed and hearing rumours of all kinds, they began to think about the match. What would happen? Those in charge started to check. They discovered that UEFA had decided not to suspend the Champions League fixtures planned for that Wednesday. In principle, the game was still to be played the next day.

Benítez tried to keep things calm and decided to go ahead as planned. He took the players out to train to relieve the tension of the journey and the horror of the brutal attack.

Some journalists, on the other hand, were more than a little terrified. Checking on the map, they discovered the relative proximity of the conflict between Russia and Chechnya and feared that at that time of international uncertainty they might be affected by the consequences of a war which, in theory, was confined to the local area.

Benítez's debut in European competition couldn't have been more eventful – though to think about football at times like these seemed frivolous. The truth was that on that tragic day the Valencia team found themselves thousands of kilometres from home, immersed in a state of profound trepidation and in a country whose communications weren't ideal. The local authorities and their hosts, the Chernomorets team, extended warm hospitality and went out of their way to look after them. For a population who were unused to watching top-flight international football the qualifying game with Valencia had been celebrated as a great event.

The team stayed the night in their base hotel, their eyes fixed on the television, especially on the international channels, and waiting to play the next day. However on the Thursday morning UEFA announced a change of plan. They had decided to suspend the planned matches as a sign of respect for the victims in New York. Benítez's expression changed. An alternative plan had to be improvised. A desperate attempt was made to leave, hiring a plane in Moscow to return home as soon as possible, given that the aircraft which was due to pick them up was not scheduled until Friday morning. At the time all international air security was affected by what had happened in the United States. It wasn't easy to fly anywhere on the planet.

There was visible agitation. Some members of the group wanted to return to Valencia without wasting a minute. The worst moment came when they were on the way to another airport because they had been assured that a plane was available. In an aerodrome from the Stalinist era, whose amenities were so filthy they looked as if they had come out of a horror story, the Valencia squad waited in vain to leave Russia, eaten up by impatience.

The long-awaited Tupolev didn't arrive and they were forced to stay an extra day. Resigned to their fate, tired and with their nerves on edge, they returned to their hotel and waited for the planned charter plane to arrive the next morning. The flight passed without incident and landed at Manises on time. That was how the nightmare ended. With an unimaginable overdose of stress before the trip, the squad and their entourage returned home after three unforgettable days on Russian soil where they would have to return the following week.

BACK TO SQUARE ONE

Benítez redrafted his preparation plans then and there. He was a day and a half away from another League commitment. The following week everything had to be repeated once again. Back to the airport, and the same long journey. When the match was finally played it was preceded by an emotional tribute to the victims of September 11th. The local fans behaved respectfully and once again showed great hospitality towards the club from Valencia. The match ended with a narrow win for Benítez's team who had finally made their debut in the tournament. The qualifying round would be decided with a feast of goals at Mestalla.

The European experience then continued with a stop in Warsaw to play against the historic Polish team, Legia. A very tough contest with enthusiastic, vociferous fans and dozens of flares thrown from the terraces. In that clash Benítez had one of his most serious outbursts of anger with his players. At half-time he read them the riot act because of their repeated lapses and their dangerously relaxed attitude. A sloppy attitude was something which drove him to despair. A number of players were astonished when he came down on them like a ton of bricks. During the half-time teamtalk the manager's face reddened and his veins swelled, he was so angry. He couldn't understand the dream-like state of mind of his players. The eventual draw gave way to a brilliant exhibition in the return game in which Valencia got through the qualifying round after scoring half a dozen goals.

It seemed as though Valencia had taken out a subscription to green and white because their next rivals were the historic Glasgow Celtic. At Mestalla the Scottish goalkeeper Douglas played magnificently to stop his team being comprehensively knocked out in the first leg. After an onslaught from Benítez's team he only let in one goal.

At that time, Benítez used to argue that his men were the best finishers of all the first division teams, though their goal difference was not in line with their offensive play. It was true that the team attacked, took more corners than anybody and shot from any position, but there was only a trickle of goals. Against the Glaswegians the trend was the same: lots of attempts, corner kicks and an oppressive command of the game, but only a narrow win. For the return match the tables were turned. Celtic tightened the screws and Valencia defended themselves as best they could. That intense duel required extra time and a penalty shoot-out. But what Benítez would never forget about Celtic Park was the atmosphere on the terraces and the rendition of *You'll Never Walk Alone* sung by the devoted fans.

What Benítez would never forget about Celtic Park was the atmosphere.

"I've never seen anything like it in my life, it's been a wonderful experience, the fans have been behind their team throughout and they have respected us. We should learn this lesson," he said emotionally after an experience not suited to those of a nervous disposition. The Valencia players received a standing ovation from the Scottish spectators and the team responded sportingly from the centre of the pitch after an exhausting battle. They still hadn't got over the bitter memory of the final in Milan but on this occasion luck came down on Valencia's side thanks to Cañizares' safe hands in goal and the heroics of Pellegrino who anxiously asked to be involved in the penalty shoot-out, scored, and so laid the ghosts of his past to rest.

The next stop on their European travels was more sedate; they came up against a surmountable obstacle, Servette Geneva. The Swiss team suited the manager in every way: an averagely demanding opponent and a comfortable journey. Valencia went through easily. Now they were in the quarter-finals and their target of a European final was tantalisingly close.

Benítez was starting to calculate. The season was coming into its final straight and their hopes for the League were intact. They had to divide their efforts. Their next opponents were mind-boggling: Inter Milan, managed by his predecessor, Héctor Cúper, and with an old acquaintance in their ranks, Javier Farinós. At the San Siro the one on one of the cursed final of the Champions League was repeating itself. This time it was a good result. In the return leg matters were complicated by an early goal from the Italians. From then on they launched an attack on Inter but there was no way they could score, despite untold missed opportunities. Toldo, the goalkeeper, was the hero for Inter although he ended up being sent off. Even then the goal didn't come. In its wake the clash left feelings of impotence and frustration. Their European adventure ended in a sad way. The next time they would take part in the UEFA Cup would be two seasons later and, despite winning it, that would also prove to be a bitter experience for Valencia far away from home.

For Rafa Benítez it was even more painful.

RETURN TO TURKEY

On Thursday 11th March 2004, Valencia were in Ankara, the capital of Turkey, to play a little-known team, Gençlerbirligi, whose excellent progress in the competition was worthy of respect. It was the second consecutive trip to the country for Benítez and his men.

Deep down the manager still remembered with rancour the death of his brother-in-law, a member of the armed forces who had been killed in a plane

It seemed that fate was determined to take him to Turkey yet again.

crash in Turkey on May 26th, 2003. He had been returning home as part of a humanitarian mission which had been to Afghanistan. A total of 62 Spanish servicemen died when their plane crashed, in strange circumstances, into a hillside near the Turkish city of Trabzon.

The tragedy rocked the whole of Spanish society. Benítez and his family were with his sister Rosario and his nephews at what was a very heartbreaking time, and at the emotional funeral presided over by the King and Queen of Spain at Torrejón airbase. That night during a long telephone conversation with me he expressed his indignation: "This is a disaster, lots of honours but they treat them any old way, what chaos, it's not fair!" He was bitter.

He had strong emotional ties with his brother-in-law, veterinary major,

The wedding of Rafa Benítez's sister Rosario and José Antonio Fernández Martínez,
who was killed in a plane crash in Turkey in 2003.

José Antonio Fernández Martínez, a football fan and friend. Now it seemed that fate was determined to take him to Turkey yet again and to remind him of what had been a very painful time.

Valencia had already knocked out Besiktas Istanbul with a goal in the last minute of the first leg played at Mestalla, even though they had been behind on two occasions, and to their serious resistance at the Inonu Stadium where they had won the return leg 2-0. They had also already played in Sweden, where the final was due to be played in the Spring, and it was a comfortable start to the competition. Against AIK Solna of Stockholm, Valencia went through with two goals, one in each of two fairly effortless matches.

Later, things became more difficult. Benítez's men choked on Maccabi Haifa, an apparently straightforward opponent, and drew 0-0 at Mestalla. There was no return leg in Israel for security reasons. After the usual uncertainty of these cases, UEFA decided it should be played at a neutral venue and Sparta Rotterdam's ground was chosen. In Holland, Valencia did everything right and won with a convincing 4-0 scoreline.

On the morning of March 11th, Benítez was thinking about an opponent who was more dangerous than many appreciated – not as famous as other Turkish teams but awkward to play against. It was then that news came from Spain of a serious terrorist attack. This time the nightmare was to be closer to home and it caught him full on. Word got round. Players, journalists, and everyone with them huddled round television sets to find out the scale of what had happened. Mobile phones never stopped.

As the hours went by details of the bombings emerged and the number of reported victims increased shockingly. Almost 200 dead, more than 1,500 injured. Staggered by the massacre, Benítez thought that it would be advisable to suspend the match. There was no will to play. He saw it as an insult to human dignity.

However, UEFA decided, just as on the day of the attack on the Twin Towers, that all planned matches should be played. Benítez was depressed, his spirits at rock bottom. He began to receive news of his closest relatives. His nephews and nieces went to a school close to where one of the explosions had occurred. Another niece was crossing a bridge close to Atocha station where a bomb had gone off and had to be treated for toxic smoke inhalation. His sister-in-law's brother had been on one of the trains. He had been hit by the shockwave and thrown out by it. Fortunately his wounds weren't serious and he was out of danger. Another relative was able to get off the train unharmed, by his side lay two dead bodies.

All the unimaginable horror struck him savagely and unexpectedly. It was beginning to seem that the number 11 was cursed. Benítez, demoralised and with no inclination to talk about football, abandoned his usual talk after the game. Days later he would take the floor:

"Politicians must sort this out, we can't carry on like this. My sister still hasn't received an explanation. After nine months I am still hearing the same message, measures must be taken, we must tighten up anti-terrorist legislation. I had advised my sister not to focus on the causes or on those who are responsible, but to think about the future and about her children. But we all feel solidarity with the victims and contempt for the murderers... we have to act."

This, in essence, was the harsh message he went public with.

It was a monologue that no journalist dared interrupt. In the deathly silence of the press room at Paterna, Benítez gave vent to all the pent-up anger and stress he felt. He was searching for an explanation for this barbaric act. The manager linked his pain for the loss of a family member – the victim of an accident – and the bad management of the authorities, with his rage for the lives lost in the terrorist attack. The players appeared before the respectful Turkish fans with a placard in which they expressed their solidarity with all the Spanish people. The match went ahead but the Valencian team were absent. The Turks won by the narrowest of margins when they scored a penalty on that unhappy night.

The competition would continue but Benítez couldn't get that day and the unfair suffering of so many innocent people out of his mind. Spanish football expressed its solidarity in many ways: the minutes of silence, black armbands, flags flying at half-mast.

In the end the routine of the competition would prevail and for Valencia it would bring a rather different type of scare. Gençlerbirligi were knocked out in extra time with a silver goal which meant Valencia went through but with more of a struggle than Benítez had expected on that cold morning in Ankara, before news of all the horror and fear had broken.

On the way to the final at the Ullevi Stadium they were to face one of the biggest teams in French football: Girondins Bourdeux. Tradition was maintained. Valencia had never been knocked out by a French club and they won both matches. Another maxim came true, Valencia had won every one of their six European semi-finals. Villarreal were to put this record to the test in a match which was charged with emotion and passion. Two teams from the Valencian region meeting for the first time in such circumstances. Paquito, a legendary name in the history of Valencia managed Villarreal. The seventh semi-final win was decided by the closest of margins with a penalty in favour of Valencia after two very closely-fought games.

Benítez was on the threshold of his first European final; his opponents, Olympique Marseille, an illustrious team who had been involved in the first stages of the Champions League and were now in the UEFA Cup, were fearsome opposition. They had knocked out Liverpool, Inter Milan and Newcastle. Benítez knew his opponents well and had studied them in depth. Valencia came to the final in exceptional form, already crowned as League

Champions. The emotional burden of the two European finals the club had recently lost didn't upset the manager too much: "There are new people and the past heals memories."

Preparation for the game was as usual, they travelled the day before, a relaxed base in the city centre, nothing out of the ordinary. Benítez avoided the habits of previous fixtures and didn't shut himself away for more time than was necessary. His only concern was the ball that would be used for the final. A very light, grey ball with an uneven flight path, on a day when a strong breeze was blowing in Gothenburg, and in a stadium that let the wind in through the end stands which were lower than the others. As confidence in their own possibilities was absolute, Benítez was sure his team would perform well; at that time they were like a runaway racehorse which has to be reined in – anxious to compete, confident about its abilities.

I'll never be better anywhere than in Valencia.

The final was decided by a penalty, when Barthez, in goal, committed a clear foul just before half-time, one which also led to him being sent off. Collina, the Italian referee, was in no doubt. Vicente opened the scoring. In the second half, Valencia played freely and Marseille couldn't overcome the handicap of being a player down. Mista finished the game off with a second goal. It all turned out perfectly. Valencia notched up their fifth European title and became the second Spanish team to win the UEFA Cup. Not since 1986 when Real Madrid had won – the same year in which Benítez had retired as a player – had any other Spanish team succeeded.

It was the third title for a manager who was living out his last days at Valencia and to whom the fans paid tribute. For the first time in their history Valencia had won two trophies in one season. At the end of the 2004 season many were celebrating them as the best team in the world.

After that, Benítez would no longer return to the bench at Mestalla.

GOODBYE VALENCIA

"I'll never be better anywhere than in Valencia." This was the phrase that was constantly repeated by Rafa Benítez.

Whenever the issue of his future arose, the same reply was always heard. Benítez was comfortable in the city. His family was too. He had strong emotional ties there since the birth of his second daughter; he identified with Valencia and its people; his attachment to his surroundings was genuine. His wife, Montse, was also settled and her contentment brought Rafa an emotional stability.

Other teams had hankered for his services for a long time. But Valencia had first and absolute preference. For the first time in his professional career he had been able to develop a serious project. Benítez, always the perfectionist, was still not completely satisfied and believed that the club could be even better if certain organisational improvements could be made. He undoubtedly wanted to finish the job.

Benítez and Valencia seemed to be made for each other. People loved him; they showed a certain affection and admiration for him. The fans had demonstrated this on more than one occasion by chanting his name on the terraces of Mestalla. His followers believed in his philosophy because the titles he had won had shattered their earlier scepticism. Now, after three years full of great moments, the vast majority agreed with his methods. The team could play by heart. Nothing seemed to stand in the way of a long relationship and, from the outside, nobody could have imagined that a manager able to win two titles in a single season would go to another club. However, that relationship progressively deteriorated until the final split occurred.

THE BOMBSHELL HITS

Early on the morning of Tuesday 2nd June 2004, Rafa Benítez called an urgent press conference at Paterna, where he was to announce his departure. There was a considerable commotion amongst the media. The news was a bombshell and it was about to explode. No questions were allowed. Rafa

Rafa poses with his coaching team in the 2003/04 season at Valencia.
Paco Ayestarán, Antonio López and José Manuel Ochotorena.

Benítez, very emotionally, read a short statement which he had prepared at home. His wife had warned him the night before: "You'd better write it down, otherwise you won't know what to say."

She was right, scarcely had he finished reading it than he burst into tears, got up and rushed to the dressing rooms, head down. The statement was brief: "I have possibly taken the most difficult decision in my sporting life: I'm not going to stay at Valencia FC next season. I positively value the club's intention to reach an agreement, but, after the events of last season, personal and emotional damage have made me reconsider staying here. On a professional level I shall take a few days to examine the alternatives open to me and make the most suitable decision. On a personal level I should like to thank everyone for their support over the last three years, the players, the club employees, the media and especially the fans. I have two daughters, one of them is Valencian and both of them are *falleras*, for this reason the city of Valencia and Valencia FC will always be in my thoughts and in my heart."

That's how the story of Rafa Benítez's time as manager of Valencia came to an end. It had been 13 years since a manager had stayed three consecutive seasons at the club – it had not happened since the departure of Víctor Espárrago. Benítez still had a year to run on his contract and were he to have stayed he would have equalled the record of the great Alfredo di Stéfano, who managed Valencia from 1970 to 1974, quite a record.

The news had a great impact. People asked why Benítez was going. There were answers to satisfy everyone. The most untrusting were quick to say that he'd had a juicy offer from another club; others that it was the right time for him to leave because it would be impossible for him to improve the performance to date. These same doubters had already decided that Benítez wouldn't be able to get Valencia to a Champions League final. In the end, with Liverpool, it was to take him only a year – and he would win.

What is certain is that the matter caught the vast majority of people off guard.

STORM CLOUDS

There had been signs of a storm brewing for some months before but the glorious end of season had led people to think that there would be some sort of compromise. The conflict reached its low point as a direct result of what had happened, or rather, hadn't happened. Although the contract between the club and its manager was up to the end of June 2005, the absence of a compensation clause was to allow the manager, under Spanish employment law, to break his contractual ties unilaterally. Benítez knew this, as did those in charge at Valencia. In March, talks had been initiated to extend and improve his contract. At that time, Valencia were still in both the competitions that they would end up winning and seemed to be on an unstoppable advance after having had a little rough patch. It was in these circumstances that talks began between Manuel Llorente, the club's managing director, and Manuel García Quilón, Benítez's agent. Both knew each other well. They had had dealings on many occasions; both signings and renewals of players such as Baraja, Mista, Marchena, Curro Torres – as well as Benítez himself. The tactic adopted by the club official was to drag things out; there was no hurry to finalise the agreement, time was on their side.

Nothing is wrong, we're talking and we want Benítez to stay.

Llorente acted dispassionately and offered a contract for only one further season. Quilón, acting with the full authority of Rafa Benítez, was irritated by the offer. It wasn't acceptable to him and he felt that the idea of 'negotiation' was more fictional than real. Seeing no point in agreeing a one-year contract he asked for at least a further two seasons. The tables were turned – in the past he had asked the club for one year and they had offered two.

Time passed, and the outlook for Valencia was looking increasingly rosier. Talks continued to be deadlocked – with no progress. Benítez was indignant because he couldn't understand why the club was unable to finalise his renewal contract once and for all. He didn't want distractions as he wanted to focus on the preparation of the team for what looked like a very promising future.

The story became ever more complicated.

Llorente was playing his game of poker, always in control, and waiting to see the final outcome of the season. "Llorente doesn't value work, only results," Benítez was to say. It was a cry from the heart about how things were getting bogged down. From the club's side, the official comments were optimistic and calm – Nothing is wrong, we're talking and we want Benítez to stay with us for many years.

Benítez didn't want to talk about it. He wanted to focus on his work.

As the days went by though he would abandon this stance and would launch his own attacks on those in charge at the club.

After winning the League in Seville, an informal meeting was held in Benítez's room in the early hours of the morning. Llorente said he couldn't offer him a longer contract because if the following year they lost three matches in a row he would have to cancel it. The slow progress imposed by the managing director reached a critical point on Wednesday, 13th May, at Villarreal. That night the local team and Valencia were playing a League match that had been brought forward to facilitate Valencia's preparation for the UEFA Cup Final.

Valencia were already League Champions and, for them, the match was a mere formality. Benítez's agent was in town because he was going to finalise the contract of the goalkeeper, Pepe Reina, and had taken advantage of the trip from Madrid to meet Llorente before the match. His intention was to also sort out the manager's continuance at the club. However, the meeting didn't take place. Valencia's managing director wasn't available as he was at a formal lunch with the directors of the two clubs. García Quilón understood this commitment and agreed to have coffee with him first thing in the afternoon.

He waited for Llorente to call him on his mobile. When it didn't ring he decided to take the initiative and call Llorente. He tried several times with no success. By mid-afternoon Quilón decided to drive back to Madrid as he had to go to a dinner that night. Finally, on a dual carriageway near Buñol, 40 kilometres from Valencia and almost 100 from Villarreal, he recieved a call from Llorente who, after apologising, suggested they still hold the planned meeting. Quilón told him that it was too late and that he had to continue his journey. The atmosphere was strained. Another failure to meet up which complicated things even further – though nothing had yet been lost.

Three days before the European final in Gothenburg, Benítez no longer side-stepped the issue. He was asked about the matter on the Channel 9 programme *Minut a minut*.

"It seems they think more of me elsewhere than they do at home. I would like to stay but it's not clear that the Valencia management want me to," he stated. He was clearly hurt.

At that time he started to seriously toy with the possibility of not completing the year he had to run on his contract. He had always wanted to continue, but now serious doubts had begun to creep in. At the club nobody took the manager's veiled threats seriously. They believed that the momentum of events would settle the matter without too many problems. The strategy bandied around was that of holding out to the last and, depending on the season's results, play one card or the other. For Benítez to leave after winning the League just wasn't contemplated. The club was going through a splendid period and a key one in terms of its development. Probably, while Llorente delayed renewing the manager's contract, behind the scenes they were deciding a matter of crucial importance – one which was of greater significance to them than that of the manager's contract, the shareholding control of Valencia.

For five years there had an ongoing conflict within the organisation as Paco Roig, a former chairman, had attempted to return to his post. Now it was coming to an end. Attempts to acquire huge numbers of shares had led to an exaggerated and totally unrealistic share price. Their face value was 48 euros, yet in the mad rush to control the club they reached a price of 600 euros. There was a fierce struggle between the previous chairman and the Bautista Soler family who came out in support and defence of the current board of directors. The wealth of the Soler family would triumph in the end. Roig sold his shares at an exorbitant price in the deal of a lifetime and disappeared from the scene.

All this was going on at the same time as the delayed renewal of Rafa Benítez's contract and the team's magnificent double. A highly charged cocktail which revealed the instability of the club's management and the impenetrability of the staff.

Preparations were being made for the arrival of those who had invested millions of euros in Valencia and had saved the fragile board, chaired by Jaume Ortí. Maybe this was a determining factor in Llorente's prudence in his talks with Benítez, but it's equally true that over the same period of time contract renewal of two star players, Albelda and Ayala, had been agreed.

Uncertainty at board level didn't stop some contracts being extended for men with modest careers, but who enjoyed great prestige among the fans. Benítez was starting to feel the effects of an apparently absurd situation. Sporting triumph would be his best argument to counter those who were waiting to weigh up the balance before taking their final step. The organisation's official approach of waiting to know the results left him greatly disillusioned. He believed that his track record and his dedication were sufficient to assess his merit. That wasn't the case. Another factor to take into account was, doubtless, the late appearance on the scene of Juan Bautista

Soler, the most powerful man at the club whose arrival, had it come a couple of weeks earlier, would have stopped Benítez's departure. Juan B. Soler, current chairman of Valencia, would have led the talks personally and would have finalised things quickly. But he arrived too late. Despite his desperate attempts to achieve a positive outcome, by the time he intervened things had gone too far. Three days after Benítez announced his departure the agreement between Soler and Roig was reached. Roig sold his shares to Soler.

THE STORY UNFOLDS

The denouement happened the last weekend of May. Rafa Benítez could stand no more. He decided to leave Valencia. He phoned García Quilón, who tried to persuade him and asked him to be calm. Despite the delays and the snub suffered, Quilón seemed to want to try again to agree a new deal. He felt that now all the cards were in Rafa's hand. Besides, the club had changed, there were new officials and new horizons were opening up.

But Benítez's pride had been hurt. García Quilón knew him well and decided to calm things down – to cool tempers. He suggested that he should take a couple of days to reflect quietly and weigh up the pros and cons. Benítez shut himself away at home with his family. He didn't answer the phone. Instead he discussed with his wife the decision that was going to change his life. On the Sunday evening he contacted García Quilón again. There was no going back, the decision was irrevocable. Things had to be resolved

Benítez's pride had been hurt.

immediately. García Quilón travelled to Valencia the next day to meet with club officials. The meeting took place at Benítez's house, where García Quilón made a last vain attempt to convince him – but it was impossible. Stubbornness is one of Benítez's most marked traits and he was completely convinced he was doing the right thing. From that moment on his agent realised that his client's future no longer lay on the banks of the River Turia and he sought to defend Benítez's interests. Rafa had the backing of his wife who, with a heavy heart, had understood her husband's reasons and had accepted his wish to leave Valencia.

On the table were four offers: two from England, Spurs and Liverpool; one from Rome and the most substantial, in monetary terms, from the Turkish side, Besiktas Istanbul.

Stubbornness is one of Benítez's most marked traits.

Over and above monetary concerns though, Benítez's priorities were the sporting issues. As he has confessed in public, he's neither a spendthrift nor is he capricious. His financial position had been difficult in earlier years, but now after the achievements of Valencia he was in a privileged position. He could choose whether or not to prioritise financial considerations. And so putting financial matters as secondary, and sporting issues as the priority, he chose Liverpool.

At half past one a delegation from Valencia FC arrived at his home – Manuel Llorente, who had to date undertaken most of the negotiations, Juan Bautista Soler, the most powerful man at the club and future chairman, who wanted to take over discussions and his right-hand man and legal adviser, Enrique Lucas.

The latter two represented the new order which was to be established at Valencia. They arrived willing to resolve matters, convinced they could wrap things up once and for all. They soon realised this wasn't to be the case. The meeting continued until five o'clock in the afternoon in a tense atmosphere, there was no letting up, not even for a frugal lunch. From the outset Benítez expressed his wish to leave and his conviction that there was no other solution. His resolve surprised them. There were moments of tension and mutual recriminations between Llorente and the manager and his agent as to how negotiations had progressed. Soler tried to keep the peace and reconcile positions. He offered the manager three more years on his contract, giving him absolute guarantees that he would be allowed to work completely autonomously and have total backing for his decisions. He also guaranteed that he could sign any players he asked for. In short, he granted him complete

Rafa Benítez with his wife Montse.

control of sporting matters. Benítez would be able to do as he wished and he could choose his colleagues. Soler explained that the club was doing better, that he was a man of his word and that he would stick to all his promises. For Soler, at that moment, Benítez was the cornerstone of his future plans.

Not even all could sway the manager.

His argument was concise: "It's too late now."

In the past, Benítez had known broken promises and he had no absolute guarantees that Soler would be true to his word. He also said that he had worked under 150% pressure and had demanded of the squad more than they were able to give.

"Another year like this would be unbearable for me and for the players."

His reproaches provoked an exchange of accusations. Benítez took Llorente to task for negotiating with other managers behind his back: Gregorio Manzano, also represented by García Quilón and César Ferrando, a Valencian coach apprenticed at Mestalla. For his part, Llorente reproached him for having offered himself to Real Madrid halfway through the season, a rumour which had come from the close circle of the Madrid chairman, Florentino Pérez. García Quilón responded vehemently. Benítez's agent provided concrete facts and names of witnesses; according to his version, it had been Florentino who, on a couple of occasions, had asked about the Valencia manager and had called on his agent to set up a formal meeting to discuss the matter. These fleeting encounters with Pérez had taken place firstly at the Bernabéu during the Real Madrid-Sevilla match, and then at the Vicente Calderón stadium at the end of the Atlético Madrid-Real Madrid derby. Both these matches, especially the second one, took place when the contest between Valencia and Madrid for the championship was at its height.

The meeting at Benítez's home lasted almost an hour, ending with the handing over of his cancelled contract and the settlement for the manager's agent which the representatives of Valencia refused to accept. The next day it was entered in the club's official records.

Later there was a private meeting in which the legal issues were finalised and agreement was reached that neither party would seek litigation in the courts. Both parties agreed to end the relationship in a friendly manner – but that intention only remained a verbal one and things were to swiftly change. Valencia took the initiative, filing a suit against Benítez for damages. The manager argued that the law was on his side and that the club were obliged to compensate him.

And so began a conflict which is still to be resolved in court.

The key people in the split, Rafa Benítez and Manuel Llorente, were for many months close colleagues. They had no difficulty understanding each other, they spoke the same language, they confided in each other. Benítez valued Llorente's professionalism. He was a valuable ally in resolving problems or getting things done. Llorente was a businessman – not from the football world – a man very different to those who usually occupy such a post in an important club. Their close understanding allowed them to support each other. Benítez has always valued rigour and professionalism, he likes everything to be well organised. Llorente is of the same creed. The manager was also very appreciative of the gesture that Llorente had made, of his own free will, to double the stipulated premium in his first season after winning the League. The passage of time and the confrontations that occurred severely damaged their relationship.

An abyss had opened up between them.

>> CHAPTER 8   **OFF TO ANFIELD**

A SPANISH ARMADA
ON THE ROAD TO THE TITLE
LUIS GARCÍA'S NIGHT
A STIFF UPPER LIP
THROUGH TO THE SEMI-FINALS

8   OFF TO ANFIELD

In June 2004 it was announced that Rafa Benítez was to join Liverpool FC. His first match in charge was to be a friendly at the end of July against Celtic, who they beat 5-1.

At the press conference Liverpool chief executive, Rick Parry, confirmed that Benítez had been their number one target: "Benítez clearly wanted to come to Liverpool and that shone out in every conversation we had… he is young, enthusiastic and hungry for success."

Benítez himself was also delighted, "It is like a dream to be here. I am very, very proud to be joining one of the most important clubs in the world, in one of the best leagues in the world – and I want to win."

It all began very well. In Benítez's first Premiership match, against Spurs, Cissé scored after thirty-eight minutes, and things were looking good. But, it was short lived, as Spurs managed to pull back a goal and hold on for a draw. Over the next months Liverpool experienced a yo-yo of results, and when they struggled against Watford in the Carling Cup and lost to Burnley in the third round of the FA Cup it was beginning to look as if life as an English manager wasn't going to be a bed of roses. And for the football pundits and other observers it was looking as if the 2004-05 season could be no more than a transitional one for Liverpool.

At the heart of Melwood, the Liverpool FC facilities which are used exclusively by the first team, are Benítez's headquarters. The club has another complex reserved for their other teams and for away teams visiting Anfield.

Benítez spends hours in a huge office with every comfort close to hand, and is well looked after by the club employees. This is a privileged space. Next door are the offices of his coaching staff. Here, Benítez, absorbed in total dedication, can often lose track of time, until close colleagues remind him that life also exists outside the office.

From behind his desk an enormous window provides a fantastic view over the training pitches, one of which is covered for those days when it rains heavily. From this private watch tower the manager can keep an eye on everything that is going on simply by raising the blinds, which also provide privacy when he needs it. Here he can choose either to shut himself away or to watch the players at work. This is something new for a man used to being down on the pitch running the training sessions. In the past, it's been rare for him to leave his fitness coach or his assistants to lead training by themselves. But this is one of the differences between English and Spanish football. In some Premiership teams there may be weeks when the manager has little contact with his players, something which was unthinkable when Benítez was in Spain.

Every day, Benítez, 'the Boss' as he is called, and his colleagues schedule the work for the team. The rate is always frantic. As 2005 was beginning and Rafa Benítez was halfway through his first season, Liverpool were still involved in four competitions. There was no let-up for them. Work hadn't stopped at Christmas, if anything it had become even more intense.

An amazing atmosphere of calm prevails.

Benítez has excellent resources to do his job at Liverpool. He's short of nothing. His own videotapes and an extensive collection of match videos are neatly stacked on several shelves – rival teams, interesting players to follow in the future, his own team's performances. Amongst them are also the videos from earlier periods in his career.

Benítez settled in well in his new surroundings. He proposed changes to some working practices which were deep rooted in the club. For him it was important to improve how things operated, to bring everything to date and to banish some practices which he saw as anchored in the past and no longer relevant.

Liverpool has a magnificent infrastructure, with many competent professionals. The chairman has given him full control. A chairman in England doesn't have the same direct involvement as Benítez was used to in Spain, he doesn't deal with the day-to-day matters, which are left to club executives.

Liverpool had gone through a period of some uncertainty in its club structure. An attractive bid had been made to take financial control of Liverpool FC and there had been much speculation in the Media about what the future might hold. The bid would have led to a change of chairman, but in the end it was rejected and David Moores was to continue in post, following a family tradition going back several decades. As far as the first team was concerned, Benítez was given complete authority. He's not just a coach in the usual sense of the word. His wide-ranging powers enable him to draw up a new model, and that is what he has been working on. It is one of his great challenges, but at the same time he cannot neglect other football matters. Signings, the progress in talks, the price to be paid, are all personally supervised by Benítez. His approval is required for everything.

At Melwood an amazing atmosphere of calm prevails. The press are only allowed in on a handful of occasions. Fans can't watch training sessions either. Consequently there are no cameras, no photographers, not even autograph hunters. Benítez can get on with his work in peace. Liverpool have provided him with the ideal location, an ample and well-equipped laboratory where he can stamp his own personal identity.

Near his office is the dining room where the players meet every day for lunch, a custom which was instituted to help improve camaraderie: a large room with self-service facilities, it also has a games area and a rest area.

On a wall in the conference room hangs a display showing the most important trophies Liverpool have won. Underneath it are stated the essential values that the club instils in its players: respect, a winning spirit, commitment to the team and complete dedication. It evokes the glorious traditions of the past – a reminder of other eras and of the men who created the legend which is Liverpool. Two above all others – Bill Shankly and Bob Paisley.

Liverpool created a style of their own which over the years would make them the strongest team in Europe. Great moments. A legend and a universal song – *You'll Never Walk Alone*. It's true, as thousands of ecstatic voices make sure to remind us from the most famous terrace of all stadiums, the Kop. There a legend began which grew over time. But Liverpool have also gone through hard times. The tragedies of Heysel and Hillsborough overwhelmed the hearts of their fans with sadness and struck a heavy blow to the club.

For years Liverpool FC had longed for those magic years, those unforgettable nights at Anfield, those exhilarating memories of four European

On the bench at Anfield with Alex Miller and Paco Ayestarán

Cups. The weight of this overwhelming history had now fallen on the shoulders of the first Spanish manager to arrive on English shores. This is not just any club, but the one which has won the most trophies in English footballing history.

Benítez is fully aware of where he is. He knew only too well what was expected. His excellent reputation had preceded him and the fans welcomed him with open arms. He familiarised himself with his new surroundings. New customs, too. Less media pressure. Fans who behave differently. Less argument over the manager's decisions. A team which was encouraged and from whom absolute dedication was demanded. Mistakes were more generously forgiven, and adverse results accepted with greater resignation.

Benítez has applied himself to learning English. He's been to England before, and to the United States, and he could already get by in Shakespeare's language with a degree of dignity. Now he faces press conferences in English with no problem at all. He has settled well into the British way of life. Everything is different; food, timetables, weather – but he knew all this and was prepared for it – he doesn't miss his life in Spain. He himself lives on the outskirts of Liverpool in a select area, whilst the majority of his colleagues have settled in the city centre, in the popular Albert Dock, the former dockside warehouses now converted to residential use, and with magnificent views.

A SPANISH ARMADA

The first team coach is Paco Herrera. For many years he trained Badajoz, for whom he also played. And from his time at Valencia, Benítez has brought with him the goalkeeping coach, José Manuel Ochotorena, and Paco Ayestarán, his inseparable fitness coach and assistant manager.

With them arrived several Spanish footballers who Benítez knew well and trusted. Initially this aroused some suspicion, however, with time the players gained the respect of the Anfield faithful – Xabi Alonso, for example, with his exquisite judgment and his control of play. Fernando Morientes, who arrived later, was to find it easier – partly because his quality as a player was already

Benítez walks up and down the coaches' area non-stop.

known. Besides them: Josemi, Núñez and Luis García completed the 'armada' which in turn led to Spanish flags appearing on the terraces, some even with the famous Osborne bull on them.

On 14th August 2004, Rafa Benítez became the first Spanish manager to lead an English league club in the Premiership. His debut was at White Hart Lane against Spurs, and the match ended as a draw. A week later came his Anfield debut. That afternoon Liverpool beat Manchester City by 2-1.

Three classic teams head the Premiership: Arsenal, Manchester United and Chelsea. In his opening season Benítez was only too aware that Liverpool were not up with them yet. He also knew that he was not going to be able to work miracles straight away (though winning the Champions League was nothing short of that). His way of working needs time and patience. He has a five-year contract and a lot of work ahead to impose his brand of football. Despite the remarkable victory in Istanbul, his team is still in a transitional stage, moving towards a new style, unbalanced in some areas, and with a pattern of play that needs to improve.

At the beginning of 2005, a spate of injuries in the squad was to make his job even more difficult. He was already working to develop the style and approach of his team, although the demands of the fixture list didn't give him many opportunities. That was something that most astonished him about English football: the number of games scheduled. A mass of them, all fought out intensely, uncompromisingly and at a diabolical speed. Referees rarely interrupt play and the pace of the players is extremely fast. No quarter is given. The keenness on the pitch infects the stands, and vice versa, until a climax of excitement is reached. The crowd roars at the slightest opportunity in support of their team.

And so it was in his first match against Liverpool's long-standing rivals, Manchester United. Benítez could be seen walking non-stop up and down the coaches' area, whilst the phlegmatic Alex Ferguson hardly moved from his seat. The Spanish manager still gestures in the same way as he did in the Spanish league – he is restless, totally involved in the game. It's not surprising that Kevin Keegan, whilst still managing Manchester City, complained sarcastically at a press conference of having missed seeing a goal "because the other manager was always standing up, blocking my view. I couldn't see."

But there are times, when the worship of the Anfield supporters doesn't stop them losing. Nor does the warning sign in the narrow tunnel leading to the pitch. The sign that reminds players, and sometimes intimidates them, that 'This is Anfield'.

This time the men from Old Trafford had played better. Behind them was a battle fought as ever with great intensity. There was disappointment amongst the fans as they left the terraces in silence.

Benítez accepted defeat: "We must improve if we want to be on top in the future, there's a long way to go yet."

He didn't beat about the bush or make excuses. His was a sensible and honest reading of the situation.

There was work to do.

ON THE ROAD TO THE TITLE

Before that magic moment of lifting the most important trophy in European club football, Liverpool's route to victory had been a long and difficult one.

Forced to play in the qualifying rounds they were faced with near disaster against the Austrian team, Graz. They had won the away leg comfortably, but they suffered an unexpected defeat at Anfield. It was a close call for Liverpool in a match which very nearly went into extra time. At the very least it unsettled the fans.

Benítez hadn't been in the job long. The team had come back from a tour of the United States where they had played a number of friendlies against other well-known teams. Now their target was clear: to be one of the 32 best teams in Europe, and then to get through to the group stages of the Champions League. After that it was just a matter of going as far as possible, without setting targets. Benítez's view was based on a realistic assessment of the potential of his team. He didn't want to mislead, or raise false hopes.

The team were in a transitional phase, but there were already some imbalances which worried Benítez. There were patches of good play, and at times they could play with an intensity which unnerved their opponents, but they didn't make the most of it. They just weren't driving home the advantage.

At home, Liverpool were adapting well, their performances had improved and they appeared at ease and self-assured. Away from home it was a different story, the team were more hesitant and much more restrained.

Benítez commented on this in Athens to members of the Spanish press who were there to cover the Paralympics. It was the eve of Liverpool's match against Olympiakos.

In the interview Rafa was very open: he was worried about the limitations that his players were showing in their matches. Benítez was committed to ensuring that they learn and absorb his approach, but patience was required, and, more than that, time; a factor which can not be influenced by willpower.

Defeat in the Greek capital made things far more difficult than had been envisaged. The day of the sixth and final game of the group matches arrived. Liverpool and Olympiakos were to meet at Anfield in a match that would decide which of the two teams would go forward to the next round. Both had everything to play for.

Off to Anfield

Urged on by their fans, Liverpool began the match as favourites but a two goal win was needed. The Anfield legend inspired optimism. It was achievable, but huge effort and absolute concentration would be required. For Rafa Benítez it was to be his first major test since arriving on the banks of the Mersey.

It was exactly how a football match should be, played as if it was a final. It was the first, but not the last, such match in their campaign. It was an epic game, full of emotion and with a spectacular comeback. The Greek champions took the lead, with a goal that hadn't been in the script of the Liverpool supporters who backed their team to the hilt. But the comeback that was to emerge was magnificent. Liverpool just had to go all out for the three goals they needed.

The equaliser gave them hope. Now their efforts intensified. A second goal. The crowd grew delirious with excitement. Now there was just one goal to score, but time was ticking away inexorably.

As Rafa watched the game he seemed to show no emotion. He stood there wrapped in his overcoat, his trademark glasses and his intense demeanour making him look the part of a university professor. Concentration was written all over his face.

And the goal came.

The match was in its dying moments. Steven Gerrard took it on himself to charge forward and, with a powerful shot from the edge of the area, he scored. Anfield exploded in ecstasy.

There was the goal that had been dreamed of. Scored in front of the legendary Kop. It was as if time had turned the clock back. Here was that eternal Liverpool – the Liverpool that never gives in, is always capable of getting a result, no matter how difficult it might seem. The miracle had been achieved. For the spectators it was as if they were reliving one of the many unforgettable nights of Liverpool history – a history of epic proportions, magic moments which live forever in the collective memory of supporters and which keep them loyal to their team even in the bad times. Gerrard may have been the goalscorer but for the thousands of fans it felt as if they too had scored that winning goal. His determination and his belief had made their wish come true, and when the ball crossed the line they went absolutely wild.

A STIFF UPPER LIP

Despite the euphoria all around him Rafa Benítez hardly batted an eyelid. His only reaction was an impulsive gesture of joy with his right arm and his fist clenched. The players piled on top of Gerrard as the noise from all four corners of Anfield grew deafening. Benítez checked the time on his watch, oblivious to that tremendous uproar. It was almost the stereotypical stiff upper lip, a supposedly British characteristic, far removed from the clichés associated with the 'Latin' temperament. Benítez was unperturbed; in his mind he had moved on to the next stage in the match. It was, after all, still not over and qualification wasn't yet guaranteed. While the Red mountain that the players had formed on top of Gerrard was breaking up, Benítez was concentrating on the certainty of the short time left. The irrepressible joy which could be felt in the ground made him anxious, the objective had still not been met. Liverpool faced those few minutes in a state of obvious over-excitement but Olympiakos could not recover. The blow had been too harsh. Liverpool's heroic achievement was now a reality, another indelible memory to be added to Anfield's copious collection.

Overwhelmed by their success, the fans couldn't imagine that the best was yet to come and that this was nothing compared to what the future held. Liverpool were still in Europe. But now they would have to wait until February 2005 for the competition to resume. Then they were to face Bayer Leverkusen, a team which had risen to considerable prominence on the European scene. A powerful club and fearsome at home, they had humiliated Real Madrid in the first stages of the competition, avenging their own defeat in the 2002 Champions League Final by the side from the Bernabéu.

Liverpool unnerved their opponents with a crushing opening.

That year Leverkusen were close to glory on three fronts. In the end the chances slipped away, with them losing decisive matches in all the three titles for which they were competing. Benítez's assessment of his opponents was moderately optimistic despite the Germans' track record. He had already seen videos of their matches against Real Madrid and had had direct reports about both encounters, reports which explained the surprising result.

"Madrid had serious lapses in concentration in Germany and paid dearly for them. Leverkusen cope well with set pieces and have a left-footed Polish player who is a great striker of the ball from outside the area," was Benítez's summary.

The man in question was Kryznowek, a player of proven quality and with the ability to shoot from any position. Benítez wasn't worried that the first leg was to be at home. On the contrary, he preferred it. Everything was analysed and planned and the manager's mental blueprint was carried out with surprising accuracy. Liverpool unnerved their opponents with a crushing opening to the game. Leverkusen couldn't cope with the home side's tempo and conceded a couple of early goals. The fans were jubilant. Gradually the Germans began to recover and, with everything seemingly lost, they threw everything into an attempt to equalise. Liverpool's momentum slowed and they adapted to the new situation. Having two goals in the bank was a great situation to be in and now Benítez's greatest worry

The fans were offering him such human warmth and so generously.

was to hold on to this advantage. Dudek's goal was beginning to be put under pressure. Leverkusen had taken a while to get into the game but now they were trying to make up for lost time. The goal came, but it was scored by Liverpool; this third one seemed to be the death sentence.

The Anfield fans couldn't believe the score. Their team had set the pace and taken their chances with breathtaking ease. The game was going to plan; even luck had been on their side. In the end, Bayer Leverkusen scored the longed-for goal after an unfortunate mistake by Dudek, which dampened Liverpool's spirits and revived the Germans' hope of winning the tie at home.

That late goal was a great disappointment and it also added uncertainty to the return leg. Rafa Benítez isn't prone to showing his emotions but on that night he experienced something which left its mark on him. It was in

Germany, in a pub near the hotel where the team stayed before the match. Rafa had gone in to watch the thrilling Champions League match between Manchester United and Milan. Before the match no-one could have foreseen that that spectacular pairing would provide the opponents against whom they would play in the final. The many Liverpool fans who were in the pub were surprised to find their manager there. Straightaway the songs and cheering began. Rafa found himself swept along by a current of warmth which touched him deeply. That very direct and close contact with the Liverpool fans opened his eyes to the true measure of the club and the goodwill they felt towards him.

There was an endless photo call which he initially bore with stoicism, but after a while with great enthusiasm, as he too became infected by the mood of happiness which was in the air. Rafa could hardly follow the match on the television screen that he had wanted to see, but other things were more important. The fans were offering him such human warmth and so generously. He had gone into their sanctuary; he was on their territory; now he was witnessing with his own eyes how they had lived the match and how they were brimming over with hope. For a man accustomed to the enforced reclusion and isolation of the typical professional it was a new experience, that immersion into the world of the fans, into an atmosphere of real comradeship. It had a huge impact on him and was an added incentive to ensure that the next day he would give them the satisfaction they yearned for.

LUIS GARCÍA'S NIGHT

Those present on the terraces of the Bay Arena at Leverkusen would not regret having come to Germany to follow their team. Liverpool played an intelligent game, and approached things in a very practical way; they didn't take risks. It wasn't long before they silenced the deafening atmosphere created by the local fans who had dreamt of going through to the quarter-finals. More than anything though it was Luis García's night. The versatile Spanish forward scored two of the three Liverpool goals and the result of the first leg was repeated. Leverkusen had no chances and they found themselves facing an opponent that blocked every route to goal. They appeared unsettled from the outset and as the game progressed, and the minutes ticked by, it became irretrievable for them. There were no problems for Liverpool who now moved on to become one of the eight best teams in Europe, ahead of other illustrious sides who had already been unexpectedly knocked out. English football had lost two of its four representatives: Arsenal and Manchester United were out though Liverpool and Chelsea had gone through. Italy was shaping up as the dominant country with three teams.

At that point Liverpool were not amongst the favourites and less so when they went through to the quarter-finals against one of the strongest sides left in the competition, Juventus. It was more than a match; it was reliving their most painful past. It was 20 years since the tragic nightmare of Heysel. Now both clubs were to meet for the first time since that fateful night and in the biggest of European competitions.

Memories of that final in Brussels were inevitable. But it was also an excellent opportunity for healing wounds; for honouring the memory of the victims and for seeking reconciliation. Those in charge of the clubs tried hard to do just that. Rafa Benítez made a comment to me once that one of the first things that had most impressed him at Anfield was the absolute silence that occurred when a one-minute silence was observed. "You can hear the rain fall." And that was how the fans responded when the entire stadium respectfully recalled that terrible event. On the terraces of The Kop a placard could be seen which paid tribute to the dead and asked for peace forever in football. The players met in the middle of the field and joined in the tribute. A few Juventus supporters present were less respectful and sabotaged things with very loutish behaviour, but they were very much in the minority.

That heartfelt ceremony paved the way for an excellent game. It was another electric start for Liverpool, urged on by the Anfield faithful, as they forced Juventus onto the defensive. It was a re-run of the match against Leverkusen; a crushing start with two goals, a spectacular one by Luis García, the other by Hyypia. It was half an hour of brilliant football, incredibly intense, overpowering a disorientated opponent. Liverpool kept the pressure on throughout the first-half and their fans were enjoying every minute. That show of power couldn't be kept up for much longer however and gradually Juventus got back into the game. The 'Vecchia Signora' began to show signs of life and to live up to their undoubted potential. Driven on by Nedved from midfield, the Italian champions pushed forward. In the end Juventus got the goal they were looking for. The result for Benítez's men was partly positive, a narrow win but with the disadvantage of having conceded an away goal. Liverpool had set the pace early on but had then lost the initiative.

In Turin, things would be very different. Interestingly, Juventus had knocked out Real Madrid in the previous round and, once again, Rafa had excellent reports about that first knock-out round match. We spoke before the match at the Delle Alpi stadium. "Rafa, they're in no hurry, they push you to the limit. Against Madrid, they wore them down first and then finished them off towards the end. Capello's sang-froid is incredible!"

That clash of two giants of European football had ended with extra time but Juventus had shown great control. The game plan was swirling around in Benítez's head; he enjoyed thinking about how he was going to face this challenge, one which had raised expectations so much. Xabi Alonso's recovery was already a gratifying reality. Liverpool began with the advantage

English football was guaranteed a place in the Final.

from the first leg but would face a hostile atmosphere and experienced opponents; they weren't going to throw everything into attack from the outset, but nor were they going to sit back. Everyone assumed that it would be a tactical match, played out by two experienced strategists.

It turned out exactly as predicted and it was Benítez who won the battle against Capello. The first step was to confuse Juventus. No sooner had the game begun than the planned four-man defence was changed to a five-man defence, with three men in midfield. Traore was added to the pair comprising the Finn, Sami Hyypia and Jamie Carragher.

The "bianco" squad got bogged down, and their men were caught up in a trap they couldn't get out of. It wasn't a brilliant match but of great interest to scholars of the game; clamorous at every turn, transmitting emotion as the minutes ticked away with no change to the score. Despite being a calculating and quick-witted team, Juventus saw how the game was slipping away from them with hardly any chance to score. They needed a goal but there was no way of overcoming an unbending, organised and perfectly positioned Liverpool who themselves could have put an end to the match with a goal on the counter-attack after a couple of excellent moves by Milan Baros.

It was thrilling to the last. A 0-0 draw gave the Reds their passport to the semi-finals. The players and the manager went over to the part of the stadium where the Liverpool fans were, several hundred of them who had created a tremendous atmosphere with their vocal backing. Benítez was radiant; he was hugging everyone, much more demonstrative than usual.

THROUGH TO THE SEMI-FINALS

With Valencia he hadn't been able to get past the barrier of the quarter-finals despite having deserved it on several occasions. This time he was through, and English football was guaranteed a place in the final. The draw produced a semi-final between the two remaining English clubs: Chelsea and Liverpool. This would be the fourth clash of the season between them: after two League games and the final at Cardiff. The omens weren't good for the Anfield side who had lost on all three occasions. But some felt that history was on their side; they were used to reaching this point, but for Chelsea it was something new, a special moment, even though they were already virtually assured of the Premiership title. There was another interesting twist to the match. On the benches sat two managers who had just arrived in the

Chelsea were overwhelmed by Liverpool's system.

UK, one Portuguese and one Spanish. Both had excellent credentials and both had won European titles in the previous season: José Mourinho with Porto in the Champions League, and Rafa Benítez with Valencia in the UEFA Cup. In addition, their teams had been champions in their respective national leagues. As well as their undoubted success, both managers had striking personalities, and were ambitious and well-known despite their different footballing backgrounds. Benítez's personality was more straightforward than Mourinho's who tended to be more controversial and occasionally bellicose. And, of course, Mourinho could resort to seemingly inexhaustible financial reserves at Chelsea. Benítez didn't have such a generous fortune at his disposal.

At this stage of the competition Rafa Benítez was already nurturing dreams of being in the final at Istanbul, though up until then he had avoided mentioning his objective. His team weren't favourites but he had no problem accepting that and it gave him the drive to overcome, once and for all, an opponent he had never beaten.

The order of the round was the opposite to the two preceding ones; he had become used to surprising his opponents first at Anfield and then winning away. The usual preference of managers in matches of this type is to play the second match at home, but given Liverpool's previous results this didn't bother him. A year earlier in the UEFA Cup semi-finals he had faced an identical situation, one which was about to repeat itself with amazing precision. Opponents from the same country in the semi-finals, and a surprise draw in the first away leg. Indeed the results were to turn out the same: the draw just as the year before at El Madrigal de Villarreal followed by a 1-0 victory at home. In both cases there was also an early goal; at Mestalla it was a penalty, while at Anfield it was even more controversial. Even more of a coincidence was that the goalscorers were players in whom Benítez had blind faith and with whom he had worked at several clubs: Mista at Valencia, Luis García at Liverpool, both fellow players at Tenerife.

The same script, the same outcome.

Chelsea had emerged as one of the best sides in European club football thanks to the investment of their owner, Roman Abramovich. Whilst they didn't have the same tradition or pedigree in this competition as Liverpool, they had already seen off two tried and tested teams of considerable prestige: Barcelona and Bayern Munich, both of whom would also become champions that year, the former in the Spanish League and the latter in the German Bundesliga.

The pressure was on Chelsea. Despite all their Premiership success some still viewed them as underdogs. They would have to show their undeniable strength to both the English football world and to the rest of European football who would be watching the match with great curiosity.

At Stamford Bridge, Benítez set up his team in a similar way to the one he had adopted in Turin. In their mission to destroy the opposition, they were to be diligent, well organised, concerned to occupy vital positions and not to concede the advantage in any area of the pitch.

Apparently a conservative tactic, it was an astute way to get the best out of his men. The two teams knew each other well, but this time if Liverpool's motivation could be greater, the result could be different to that of the previous clashes. There was a lot at stake. Xabi Alonso was to come face-to-face with Frank Lampard after the serious injury suffered by the Spanish midfielder at Anfield on the first day of 2005. Alonso didn't come off very well from this encounter either. The referee cautioned him in the second half and the yellow card stopped him playing in the return leg.

Twenty years since their last final. Now Liverpool were back.

Before that, a fierce battle was fought, as had been the case against Juventus; Chelsea were overwhelmed by Liverpool's system which gave them no breathing space. There was a constant cut and thrust but unlike Cardiff there were no goals. The 0-0 final score was an excellent result but it was still a little dangerous. A Liverpool goal at Stamford Bridge would have forced Chelsea to score two at Anfield.

At Anfield all the cautiousness that had been shown in London was gone. Now, with their fans behind them, they were taking risks. The stadium was in party mood as the Liverpool players came on to the pitch, determined not to let their fans down. They immediately forced the pace of the match. It was a changed team, repeating the early pressure that they had shown in their matches against Leverkusen and Juventus. This was the other side of Liverpool, a vibrant and intense style of football, which set alight the spirits of the bursting terraces.

The long-awaited goal came. First there were appeals for a penalty and then confusion as to whether the ball had gone completely over the line. The referee and his assistant gave it and the crowd erupted. This early goal from Luis García had now tilted the balance of the match. Chelsea felt the sting but there was still time, plenty of the match was still to be played, and it was clear that Liverpool were missing the natural flow to their play that their midfield play-maker, Alonso, would have given.

Benítez had anticipated this and knew that his men would have chances to counter-attack as Chelsea turned up the the pressure. That was the key to it. The atmosphere in the stadium intensified as the game moved towards its conclusion. Liverpool defended tooth and nail; Mourinho's men were desperately trying to score. In the dying minutes they had perhaps their best chance of the match, with a powerful attempt by Eidur Gudjohnsen. It went inches past the post and Anfield held its breath.

Benítez, in his grey checked suit, white shirt, red tie, stood in desperation on the side line. The match was coming to an end with an epic intensity. The anxiety and desperation of the fans of both clubs was clear for all to see.

Then time was finally up. The whistle blew. In the stands, the response of the fans was amazing as they passionately showed their appreciation. Unforgettable moments of overwhelming emotion. Flags, scarves and chants engulfed Anfield.

Twenty years since their last final. Now Liverpool were back, for their sixth, in this most prestigious of competitions. Rafa Benítez and Mourinho greeted each other respectfully. Benítez, for his part, could hardly enjoy the party on the pitch, but his players revelled in the collective ecstasy of their fans and thanked them for their support. These were magic moments, accompanied as always by the 'hymn' of Anfied, *You'll Never Walk Alone* – the song that expresses, like no other, the fans' absolute love of their club.

>> CHAPTER 9   LIVERPOOL GLORY

A PREMONITION IN THE EARLY HOURS
AN UNUSUAL BET
THE THREE FRIENDS
AN EPIC NIGHT
THE WORST IS YET TO COME
LIFTING THE GLOOM
INTO EXTRA TIME
BETWEEN THE POSTS
THE HEROES RETURN

9   LIVERPOOL GLORY

Often, on the eve of momentous matches, I would speak to Rafa to find out his thoughts. It was a sort of custom which allowed me to understand his concerns, his intentions, how he viewed an opponent, and what cards he had up his sleeve.

I remember conversations before matches which were critical for Valencia, where they had everything to play for. That visit of Arsenal to Mestalla to decide which team would go through to the quarter-finals in the Champions League; the frustrated attempt at a comeback against Inter Milan; stellar clashes against Madrid and Barça; the UEFA Cup Final and other games like these which raise huge media expectation and prompt greater curiosity in journalists.

Benítez was fond of using an expression which he often repeated, one which attracted my attention. Every time I asked him his opinion about a match of this kind he would reply with the same word – 'winnable'. A simple term coined by a manager who would then go on to dissect all the factors of the match with the precision of a surgeon.

'Winnable' meant that, no matter how intense the hype that surrounded the match, he firmly believed his team could win if things were done the way he saw them. There was no such thing as an impossible match. He always had a wide range of options no matter who the opponents were, or the intrinsic difficulties of the contest. Rafa Benítez would, with incredible calmness, wait for the moment of truth: he never lost his composure; he was always sure of himself and nothing perturbed him. All he worried about was whether his team would do things well, and whether they would keep to the script that he carried inside his head.

Three days before the Istanbul final we spoke by phone. The conversation was much the same as usual with its analysis of all the possible things that could happen. Again the word cropped up, though it was me who said it first: "Are you going to tell me as you always do that this game is winnable too?"

Rafa smiled, remembering other conversations: "Yes, it's winnable if we do things right." He never changed his view but this time it was nothing less than the Champions League Final which awaited him as manager of Liverpool. In the fifty years of the competition only three Spanish managers had managed to lift this most important European trophy: Vicente Del Bosque, Pepe Villalonga and Miguel Muñoz. Benítez now had the chance to be the fourth, and as manager of a club that was in pursuit of its fifth European Cup.

He shook off the weight of history; although he was aware of what was at stake in Istanbul on 25th May 2005, he didn't want to give it too much importance. Some coaches advocate the need to just enjoy these matches – matches that are never to be forgotten by the players and the fans – a pinnacle of achievement, and a time when they can feel themselves to be at the centre

Rafa Benítez would, with incredible calmness, wait for the moment of truth.

of the universe. In the moments prior to the 1992 final against the Italian team Sampdoria, Johan Cruyff told his Barcelona players in the dressing room at Wembley: "Go out and enjoy yourselves."

The legendary managers of Liverpool, Bill Shankly and Bob Paisley, took a similar approach, simplifying as much as possible their messages to the players before important games. These are moments of anguish and absolute tension, when a footballer is rendered powerless by nerves, which weaken his legs and press on his stomach. It's an effective device to calm players, playing down the importance of the match; at the end of the day it's just another encounter in which each footballer has to bring out the best in himself and not be overwhelmed by the importance of what is at stake. The manager must always exude an air of serenity and control of the situation; if he is dragged along by the current of panic which these clashes generate and his men detect it, it sets a very bad example. Rafa Benítez was aware of what the match against Milan meant but he didn't want to be swallowed up by the maelstrom of the final.

His speech was no different to the usual: with the same guidelines and his in-depth analysis of their opponents, his stress of their weaknesses – a way to boost the confidence of his own players so as to get the best out of them.

There are no grandiloquent expressions, just a concern that the advice each footballer receives is applied. The setting itself will take care of pumping up the adrenalin; the pressure of these occasions is inevitable. Twenty years after that infamous final at Heysel, Liverpool were to be present again at that great event, the most sought-after final in European football.

True to tradition the team would play in red as they had done on all previous occasions since the magic night of their first win in 1977 against Borussia Mönchengladbach in the old Olympic Stadium in Rome. A year later they would face Bruges at Wembley, then a break before the fixture against Real Madrid at the Parc des Princes in Paris at the beginning of the new decade. Then finally in the mid-1980s their last European crown, again in Rome, this time against the hosts.

They had come out on top in all their finals, sometimes brilliantly, at other times after having pushed themselves to the limit. The aura of victory had enveloped the Anfield club each time until the terrible tragedy in Brussels.

Twenty years had gone by since then. Now for the Liverpool fans it was like travelling back in time to those marvellous years to relive the moments of happiness of the team which had marked an era in world football when English clubs had taken over Europe. The achievements of Liverpool were followed, to a lesser extent, by Nottingham Forest and Aston Villa. But two decades had now passed and everything had changed, even the name and the rules of the competition, though it still remained faithful to its initial intentions. It had been a long haul, full of problems and hard times, characterised by mediocrity at times, and a long way from the prominence which the Liverpool tradition demanded. There were also happier times, times which augured well for the re-launching of the club, such as their 2001 title wins under the management of Gerard Houllier. In the end though they didn't quite make the mark, that definitive step wasn't taken, and they continued to miss out on the most glorious of occasions.

The final promised to be an extremely interesting game. Two classic teams head-to-head in an unprecedented clash. Liverpool and Milan had never played each other despite their long traditions and their brilliant trophy collections. The Italians were the favourites, but this didn't worry Benítez. As he said: "Milan are the favourites, but for us just being here represents success."

In hindsight this is true. Liverpool had more than surpassed themselves by getting to Istanbul after having beaten Juventus and Chelsea, who were both League champions in their respective countries. It was a team that had been plagued by injuries – injuries which had devastated the whole squad, including its most vital members, on paper their best men. It was a team with limited resources, unable to play their brilliant signing during the winter transfer window, the forward Fernando Morientes, a man seemingly blessed in a competition in which he had played four finals and won three titles. The team had dealt with all these obstacles and, against all the odds, had got to the final. Once there, only one step remained, the last and most important one, but the most difficult.

Nobody wanted to be a bystander, nor did they want to fail. Strengthened by the demands of the quarter-finals and semi-finals, the team had acquired a marked capacity to keep going, and they had a belief in their strengths. These games against illustrious opponents, who were theoretically superior in strength, had fuelled in Benítez's men an ambition to win against all the odds. They had shown that they were inferior to no-one, that they could stand up to any opponent, and in any circumstances. The wind was in their favour and was driving their ship forward with great vigour. Benítez knew it and knew the advantages. Man for man Milan were better but Liverpool

Milan are the favourites, but for us just being here represents success.

had other strengths that they had to exploit, strengths which would enable them to win the match. Given the results they had already achieved, the players had been convinced by the manager's talk.

"They get tired, in the second half they deteriorate considerably and we can hurt them through the middle of their defence if we are able to exploit our weapons."

This was his summary diagnosis of the weak points of Ancelotti's team. Milan had run out of steam in Serie A and had lost a closely fought battle against Juventus after a thrilling contest for the 'Scudetto'. Benítez gathered as much information as possible about the team from Lombardy.

"An unstoppable machine if we let them play, players of such quality that they can make decisions for themselves. We haven't got that, but we have cards up our sleeve too," was Benítez's sincere confession. For him it was a matter of his team taking control of the match.

Experience was also on the 'Rossonero' side, champions in 2003 and with a good number of finals played since the end of the 1980s. Preparation for the match was surrounded by great anticipation. This would be a top quality final which the whole continent would be watching. The clubs represented the top two footballing powers, but the match would also be followed passionately in other countries. Rafa Benítez is the standard-bearer of an illustrious club which, in just one year since his arrival, has taken on a new lease of life. And under his leadership, a number of Spanish footballers have arrived in the UK.

Benítez had a glorious three-year period at Valencia and this caught everyone's eye. If anyone had any doubts about him then Liverpool's presence in the Champions League final has dispelled them. It has confirmed his talent and his capacity for work. All the Spanish sports media focused on the game and in particular on the Anfield club. Spain was behind Liverpool, not just because they were becoming an increasingly attractive team but also because they were seen almost as Spain's own representative. It had been a disappointing year in the competition for Spanish football. The four teams to

Benítez calculates, reflects, deduces.

go through had witnessed more downs than ups. Deportivo and Valencia didn't get through the first mini league; Barça and Madrid didn't get beyond the round of eight. A resounding failure after years of near domination. Liverpool were left; a classic English club seen almost as a Spanish Ambassador with many of its players and its manager from various parts of Spain. There was a clear interest amongst Spanish fans. They wanted to watch the game and know what Benítez's squad were going to do against a fearsome opponent; a team whose legend was more than deserved, a club with countless triumphs, a much admired team.

Benítez calculates, reflects, deduces. One of his conclusions is that it is

Liverpool Glory

essential that his team should grow as the game goes on and gain confidence whilst their opponents begin to succumb to doubt.

Liverpool would be hoping for a positive and aggressive game, one in which Milan would feel uncomfortable on the pitch and wouldn't be able to move freely. If Milan were given freedom then the likelihood of coming out of the match on top was zero. Defence would be a priority, absolute concentration would be required, never losing their shape. The formation had to be balanced. A mistake, a lapse in concentration, could cost them dearly. If the game became an uphill struggle they would have to redouble their efforts, but then Milan would find themselves in the perfect position to counter-attack and win the match. Any of their strikers could win the game with a single move. They had more than enough resources in attack. Shevchenko, Hernán Crespo, Kaká would become the greatest threats, and it was essential that they be neutralised.

The Final of the Carling Cup had already shown Liverpool's fighting spirit. Against Chelsea at Cardiff, Benítez had his first great experience of English football. The atmosphere had impressed him; the players' and the fans' commitment. He had been a hair's breadth from taking the title, after an agonising final which had gone into extra time. The parallels with the Istanbul final were similar, but this was a far more important game. At the Millennium Stadium it was as if an honorary title was at stake, with Mourinho and Benítez disputing the right to be seen as the best foreign manager, both aiming to win a title in English football in their debut year. In the end, Mourinho had won after a thrilling contest. At Cardiff, Liverpool scored first; they did so early but in the end lost. A final is a different type of game, difficult to control from the bench. It can be a fight of epic proportions, often exhausting for a team, and one in which the ability to resist can prevail over technical superiority.

A manager may be in charge but football is full of surprises. There are no margins for error, sometimes everything can go up in smoke and nothing goes according to the planned script. That is exactly what happened on that unforgettable night in Turkey. After days of exhaustive and methodical work, of conscientious preparation down to the very last detail, the turn of events led to scenes of chaos. Everything came apart almost immediately.

A basic principle in Benítez's manual was ignored in the very first minute.

A PREMONITION IN THE EARLY HOURS

A person's destiny is subject to whim and coincidence.

For Rafa Benítez, chance was once again to take an ironic twist. Turkey would again feature as it had on that anxious day of 11th March 2004, when Rafa Benítez had been in Ankara and Spain had suffered its worst ever terrorist attack; or on that sad day in June 2003 when his brother-in-law had been killed in the plane crash near Trabzon.

For the third consecutive year Rafa Benítez's progress was linked to the Ottoman nation. This time though it was a little different. Here, in Istanbul, was the chance for him to finally receive proper acclaim as a manager: the final of the Champions League, the dreamed-of game, the peak of club football, absolute glory.

Benítez jealously guarded his thoughts. He kept them to himself, they were not for public consumption. Here was a man who was protecting his personal feelings; a man who is only occasionally overwhelmed by emotion but one who does have a sensitive side and is vulnerable like any other human being. And so, the comments that he made on the days leading up to the big match were strictly about football; he concentrated on it totally and didn't want to be affected by any of the personal matters which could at any time plague him. But it didn't stop him having a mix of strange feelings that were even difficult to share with his most intimate circle.

It was in Turkey that his family had been dealt their hardest blow.

It was in Turkey that his family had been dealt their hardest blow, their worst misfortune – the death of his brother-in-law, José Antonio. Now, in that very same country, Rafa knew that he could experience the greatest joy of his footballing life, the culmination of so many years of effort and sacrifice. His prize for all the hard work he had done and all the obstacles he had overcome.

A trophy, even the UEFA Champions League trophy, couldn't wipe away his memory of the death. The resentment was still there, but at least it could help to alleviate the heartrending grief which it had entailed for him and his family. To win with Liverpool would be the best way to honour his memory, it would be a homage. José Antonio's spirit would be with him on that unforgettable night.

AN UNUSUAL BET

It was less than 24-hours before the final. Everything was under control. After the final training session at the stadium, Rafa Benítez had returned to the Crowne Plaza Hotel and had been chatting to his Spanish friends. He was just saying goodnight and was waiting for one of the four hotel lifts. An everyday occurrence in any hotel, apartment or office block, with their continuous flow of people.

As Benítez stood there he had no idea which lift would be the first to open its doors onto the ground floor. But now he suddenly felt as if he were sitting at a table in a casino. It was as if knew which card would come up, which slot the roulette ball would roll into after its many turns – red, black, odd, even.

If this lift comes down first we'll win the final by penalties tomorrow.

Maybe it was one of those totally illogical premonitions which many of us have, those crazy bets that we place with ourselves. They are all chance – a particular colour, a particular set of circumstances – situations unrelated to anything, but which superstition connects as if there were an infallible link.

"If this lift comes down first we'll win the final by penalties tomorrow," Benítez said pointing to one of the four lifts. Seconds later, the one he had chosen opened its doors. The three he had eliminated stayed shut.

Rafa gave a brimming smile to his surprised companions and disappeared off to the solitude of his room. It was as if some occult force had offered him an insight into what awaited, though not even that moment of rewarded intuition could have led him to expect the sort of final that he was about to live through.

For Emilio and Teo, the friends with whom he had enjoyed several hours of intense conversation and who had been witnesses, this was a perfect example of the Rafa Benítez they knew. No doubt if another lift had arrived before the one he had chosen he would have responded with something along the lines of: "Good, we won't need the penalties; we'll win the match before that."

And so with that premonition he said goodbye to his friends; it was the last time he spoke to them before the match. Their next meeting would be twenty four hours later when Benítez and his men had written another page of football history in letters of gold.

It's still surprising, however, that such a conscientious man, one so methodical and so unbelievably keen on planning and organisation, should have made such a bet with himself. Benítez is someone whose belief in the rational is almost Cartesian, yet he could still open himself up to the designs of chance on the eve of the most important match of his life.

He wasn't, of course, changing his principles or his convictions. It was just a form of light relief, a moment of relaxation, as complicit as a wink. And it was aimed at his friends, people who had known him from his humble beginnings, and who had followed his progress, his disappointments, his failures and also those successes that had catapulted him to fame.

He was challenging fate with an innocent game, a joke from someone shedding his role as the serious man who is always faithful to the same script, one who was now trying his luck as a fortune teller. Far away from his players and the relentless pursuit of the media he was daring to predict what would happen. In public his remarks would remain, as always, based on an exhaustive analysis of all the circumstances which could come together in a match.

THE THREE FRIENDS

The old city of Constantinople is full of symbolism, a crossroads of cultures bridging civilisations, a link between seas and continents. In the early hours of the last Wednesday in May, Rafael Benítez spent the time before the match with his closest associates, his inner circle. Teo Escamilla and Emilio García Carrasco had travelled from Madrid to Istanbul on the morning before the match. Both shared the dream of being there to see their friend, Rafa Benítez, get the moment of glory he deserved.

The Liverpool team's hotel was subject to strict security and even for Teo and Emilio it wasn't easy to get in. The three finally met after the dinner which the Liverpool players and manager had held in a private dining room. It was an emotional moment. There were warm embraces, words of encouragement, declarations of hope for Liverpool to win and a feeling of inexplicable joy. The road that Rafa had travelled to get that far had been very long. Now, thousands of miles from home, after so many shared dreams, three friends met up again, overwhelmed by the strength of their feelings, though Rafa did his best to conceal his with humour.

The three were now in the hotel bar. Every now and again Liverpool fans would approach respectfully to ask for an autograph and give Rafa their support, wish him luck and thank him for all the happiness he had given them. At another table, not far off, sat Dudek, the goalkeeper, with members of his family.

Fans would approach respectfully to ask for an autograph and give Rafa their support.

Rafa doesn't drink but that didn't stop him nibbling from a plate of nuts and dried fruit next to his friends' drinks. He ate almost compulsively.

Rafa's mobile phone never stopped ringing. It was non-stop with calls and text messages. Most were from Spain, where the most important radio stations have their main programmes at around midnight. Rafa usually prefers to cut himself off from these to avoid becoming a slave to the media. On this occasion however he had agreed in advance to record a couple of interviews that would go out after midnight on the Iberian Peninsula.

It's impossible to deal with so many calls. They wanted to talk about everything to do with football, and inevitably about the match. He had decided on his line-up except for one position: centre forward. In the end Milan Baros was chosen, a decision that Benítez would not take until the very last moment. The Czech forward had, at that time, reached an agreement to sign for Valencia which subsequently didn't happen. The manager was aware of all this and had weighed up the pros and cons of including him in the starting line-up.

Harry Kewell was also in the side, a big surprise that nobody had expected. Kewell had been recovering from an injury but had seemed to be fit, had trained well and the coaching team had faith in him. His presence was every bit a statement of principle: Liverpool were to take a more attacking approach and would have greater strength on both wings.

The bar table was suddenly turned into a figurative field of play.

Before them stood a daunting opponent, Milan, the team that Benítez had so much admired when he had started out, the one which he always referred to. In the full heat of debate, the conversation turned to the tactical movements that would be needed to come out on top. The bar table was suddenly turned into a figurative field of play. In the mock-up, glasses, beer bottles, keys and even watches were used to represent the players in what was, to the neutral observer, a complex and confusing assemblage.

Benítez began his dissertation: "They attack like this, they defend like this, this is the way they take free kicks, this is how they take corners …" a long list of planned moves and their corresponding prepared responses. Benítez had analysed his opponents from top to bottom. Nothing was left to chance. But that was nothing new.

Milan's style of play is well-known. Yet despite this, and all his exhaustive preparations, Benítez knew one thing: however much you study an opponent, there are aspects of the game which are completely uncontrollable for a manager and individual quality can shine through at any time. All he could do was hope that inspiration and good moves would be lacking from Milan.

It had been an intense week but Benítez had tried to make it as normal as possible, just like any other, so that his players wouldn't be stifled by the pressure. Teo and Emilio asked him if he really believed he could win. Rafa's reply was positive, though certain basics had to be observed if the outcome was not to be as expected, in favour of the Italian champions.

"It's very important that they don't score against us too soon and that they don't surprise us from a set piece."

Steven Gerrard and Rafa Benítez celebrate their extraordinary victory.

In the end, an erratic start to the match would shatter his careful preparation. Everything would be up in the air almost before he had sat down on the bench. The worst nightmares were coming true. It was a calamitous start and one which would test both the manager's and the players' ability to respond.

The night before the great day, Rafa Benítez, even in his wildest dreams, could not have imagined what the next day held for him at the Atatürk Stadium.

The lively conversation between the friends now turned to memories of the past, nostalgic moments when Rafa and Teo had been team mates in the Spanish second division B. Emilio also recalled the many hours when he and Rafa had shared the microphone as television commentators. Rafa's role had been more one of technical commentator who analyses the progress of the matches in detail. It was at the time when he himself was waiting for a chance to manage, a time when he knew exactly what he wanted to do. Eventually all his solid preparation would be rewarded.

Benítez's perfectionism came to the fore when, in the process of correcting his friend Emilio's construction of an English sentence, he himself made an error. Rafa was annoyed with himself and confessed to his friends his helplessness at expressing his ideas fully because of the language barrier. He admitted that this was something that he wanted to improve so that his players could get their instructions without any impediment. As with the majority of top teams, the Liverpool dressing room comprises players from many different parts of the world, though now Rafa always uses English except when giving instructions to the Spanish players. Since his arrival in England he has worked hard to improve his knowledge of English so that it will not hamper him in any way.

Hours go by. Rafa, Teo and Emilio have been sitting around the table for four hours. In other circumstances they would stay for many more. A cleaner appears and begins to polish the bar floor. It is time to say goodnight, to sleep and to have those dreams so full of hopes and fears.

On the seventh floor of the hotel, in the room next to Rick Parry, the Liverpool Chief Executive, Rafa Benítez gets into bed, ready for sleep, and the next day's final.

A phrase he often uses comes to mind: "It's just a game of football."

It's a way of playing the contest down; of making light of the moment they are all about to experience.

AN EPIC NIGHT

Deathly silence, general detachment, you could cut the tension with a knife.

That was the almost mystical aura that filled the Liverpool dressing room during their interminable wait before the last match. Confined in a large and functional room at Istanbul's Atatürk stadium on the last Wednesday of May 2005, the coaching team and the players were focussed on the game against AC Milan. This was the fixture that attracts all the attention; the holy grail of European football, the one with the most prestige and the most honour.

Liverpool, as always, were in good company. Thousands of fans had travelled with them to Turkey; not an easy or comfortable trip, but this didn't bother them too much, to be close to their team at a moment like this was worth any sacrifice. On the terraces they outnumbered the Milan fans and cheered on their side tirelessly. Rafa Benítez and his men knew their fans would be behind them all the way. What they didn't expect was just how much their loyalty and optimism would be tested.

Before leaving the hotel for the stadium a video session was arranged. First a tape was shown dealing with the tactical aspects of the game.

"These are the major problems that we're going to encounter and these are the most appropriate solutions," was the basic theme of the video, a sort of practical 'how to tackle the final guide'. It was an attempt to calm the players and build their confidence; to show them the best responses to predictable situations. It wasn't designed to pressurise them with too much information, but rather to show some basic concepts.

According to Murphy's Law if anything can go wrong, it will.

The other video was very different. A vibrant 10 minute tape, with music by the Beatles, evoking the most glorious pages in the history of the Anfield club: a gallery of decisive goals, finals won, unforgettable images which provoked emotion and a sense of the fans loyalty. It wasn't designed simply to be motivational but to reward the current inheritors of those legendary teams with the memory of happy moments – of a team with a particular way of doing things and a particular understanding of football – conveying to the current players the pride that is Liverpool. In that moment the emotional intensity reached a peak; the players knew that for them the doors of history were being opened wide.

Perhaps in the future they too would be the actors in a similar film; the role models for future generations. It was the final message about the match – what it meant and represented. From that moment on everybody would focus on the Final. Accompanied by a police escort, they made their way to the ground. On the team coach a tape played contemporary music interspersed with radio accounts of the high points the team had reached in that year's Champions League. The last chapter was still to be written.

Benítez had wanted to keep to a familiar routine in preparation for the final; he wanted to remove the pressure from his men. He had been cool, somewhat distant, when, in the training session the day before the match, he had become aware of the tremendous motivation that all his players were showing. They were going all out for it with absolute commitment in everything they did, trying to show that each and every one of them was capable of playing in the final. This was what the manager expected from his players; it was the guarantee of commitment and focus but at the same time it worried him that they were carrying such a heavy sense of responsibility. Their opponents had played more matches like this. Both the individual and the team achievements of the Milan players were overwhelmingly superior to those of Liverpool. This worried Benítez. His team just weren't as experienced.

Now was the moment.

First, the welcome chants during the warm-up and then the official finalists' parade, then the kick-off. Within the first minute reality hit hard, it was a bombshell. Paolo Maldini, captain of the Italian champions and the player who best represents their glorious run, surprised everybody with an unexpected goal. Even Maldini couldn't believe what he'd done. The Liverpool coaching staff tried to remain positive: "It's better they score early. Now the nerves have gone, it will be a different game. We'll be more relaxed."

It was a fair comment. The inevitable fear, which grips players in the early minutes of a match, is the same as the one boxers suffer during the opening rounds of a bout. Now though everything was up in the air. Liverpool were already playing under pressure, with the score against them right from the start.

Benítez felt the blow but kept calm, he was sure of his approach and firmly convinced that the team would react positively.

THE WORST IS YET TO COME

But setbacks were to come at breakneck speed. Harry Kewell had impressed the manager and had been included in the starting line up but, after scarcely 20 minutes, it all fell apart for him. The Australian's injury was troubling him and he had to leave the pitch. Kewell was devastated.

And so, the first substitution had to be made. On came Vladimir Smicer to play in the midfield, with Gerrard moving up front to link up with Baros, supported on the wings by Riise and Luis García.

According to Murphy's Law if anything can go wrong, it will. Something happened in the Italian goal area which looked like a penalty. A defender had handled the ball whilst on the ground. The Spanish referee, Mejuto González, who Rafa knows very well and whose appointment had been looked on favourably, didn't see it, though to be fair even the later television replays didn't clear up the matter. Milan moved into a rapid counter-attack and straight away Hernán Crespo scored the second Milan goal. From a possible penalty, and the chance to equalise, Liverpool had now gone one goal further behind. Now the gap was considerable. These were the worst moments for Liverpool and the best for a mighty Milan who now seemed to be controlling the game. Liverpool were no match for them; they seemed doomed to humiliation whilst Carlo Ancelotti's men were playing brilliant football.

When half-time came nobody thought that anything could be done.

Then Crespo scored yet again. It was the icing on the cake for Milan who were crushing the opposition. The Liverpool fans looked on, resigned to a massive defeat.

It wasn't the first time that Milan had taken their opponents apart in a European Final. Steaua Bucharest received a battering in a 4-0 defeat at the Nou Camp in the 1989 competition. Barcelona also suffered an identical punishment five years later in the Olympic stadium in Athens. This match was going the same way. Liverpool were becoming the whipping boy, and the worst forecasts were being confirmed.

At that point Benítez might well have wished that he had the option of calling 'time-out' to halt that maelstrom which was swallowing up his team.

When half-time came nobody thought that anything could be done, though there were still some, though very few, fans who seemed to be oblivious to the reality and who still had faith in a comeback that would raise everyone's crestfallen morale. Such was the case with Lali, the wife of goalkeeping trainer José Manuel Ochotorena. She was convinced that Liverpool would respond and said so insistently to the wives of Benítez, Paco

Ayestarán and Paco Herrera who were with her in the main stand. It's true to say though that her optimism was not generally shared.

LIFTING THE GLOOM

Inside the dressing room the long faces of the players gave away the gravity of their situation. There was a clear signal from the manager: there was still half the match to be played. He asked them to use their heads and not to be dragged down by the scoreline.

Now Benítez prepared a substitution. He told Traore to get changed and ordered Dietmar Hamann, the reliable German midfielder, who had been in the team in the semi-finals against Chelsea, to start warming up. However, that substitution didn't take place because of an unforeseen circumstance: Steve Finnan just couldn't continue despite his desperate wish to play the second half. The doctor advised that he be withdrawn given the probable risk of an injury. Benítez made an adjustment; he listened to the doctor's advice and decided to take Finnan off. Now Traore got ready to play again. Hamann was also completing his warm-up. The problem was solved; an essential tactical adjustment was made. The defence was reduced to three men and the central midfield area was strengthened.

The terraces roared the chant: "We're gonna win 4-3."

Support from fellow players was essential for the team to recover; all of them had to play their part. The half-time interval was coming to an end and the mood had improved, the players' expressions had changed. Someone mentioned the memorable game that they had played against Olympiakos. Now Liverpool had to score three goals just as they had against Olympiakos, and given that it had happened at Anfield then why couldn't it be repeated here. The optimism was contagious.

Benítez's words were simple: play and score quickly. Then it would be game on and time to attempt heroic deeds. There were no recriminations, just encouragement. Everything he said was constructive. The ultimate support though came when Liverpool appeared back on the pitch again. The reception from their fans was tremendous. The terraces roared a chant dominated by: "We're gonna win 4-3." With this show of loyalty the players had no option but to throw every ounce of effort into it.

The second half began; the game changed. Milan had given their all; now they had lost their intensity. The initiative had been given back to Liverpool who were now rallying. Benítez had asked for an early goal and it came thanks to a spectacular header from Steven Gerrard, who was leading by example. The quick flick with his head, the decisive finish, was the fuse for the chain reaction which followed.

It was as if Liverpool had been unleashed. Then the miracle occurred.

Liverpool believed that the miracle was possible and that they had a moral obligation to achieve it any way they could. Their players seemed to grow, driven on by a singular conviction. The Italians had a comfortable lead but now they were uncertain what to do, whether to attack or defend. Their indecision contrasted dramatically with the momentum of their opponents. It was as if Liverpool had been unleashed and the fans in the terraces never stopped pushing them on. Then the miracle occurred.

Smicer had known for two weeks before the final that his future lay outside the club. Rafa had told him personally. A very fit player, and technically gifted, he always seemed to be a player who never quite achieved what he was capable of. But for Liverpool he couldn't have found a better way of saying farewell. He took control of the ball in front of the area and, from just outside, launched a powerful, sharp shot on target. The goalkeeper couldn't reach it.

It was a goal. Liverpool's second.

The effect was devastating. Liverpool were flying, they had become unstoppable, Milan, on the other hand, had gone into shock, they weren't reacting, astonished by such a radical change. The Liverpool fans saw their faith rewarded but there was still a third goal needed.

It came from a penalty.

When the Spanish referee pointed to the spot, a jubilant and overpowering roar went up from the Liverpool fans. In seven magical minutes a game, which had seemed irretrievably lost and which had looked like ending up in a resounding feast of goals against them, had been turned around. All that was left was for the penalty to be taken. Xabi Alonso stepped up and shot to the right of Dida. The Brazilian goalkeeper added to the tension and emotion by parrying the ball but he couldn't prevent Alonso's follow-up from hitting the back of the net. Now Liverpool had drawn level.

Bedlam – in the Istanbul stadium, in Liverpool, in the pubs of England, in the bars of Benidorm, the Canaries, Majorca, the Costa del Sol – wherever there were football fans the reaction was one of almost disbelief. Nobody could remain indifferent when faced with such a remarkable show of determination. This was a final that would go down in history.

In football, as in life, everything is possible. Here was further tangible proof of this. Benítez, serene, standing on the sideline, took in the sudden resurgence. The quality of his men, the support of the fans, the change in the system, the relaxation of his opponents, these were the ingredients which had come together to create this metamorphosis.

Now what? It was as if Liverpool had lost contact with reality; they had been plunged into an ecstasy which had allowed their players to almost fly across the pitch. It had been contagious, something that had affected them all. Now with their objective achieved things began to settle down again, but the danger was that that level of physical exertion would inevitably have repercussions.

Nobody was basking in their heroics; there was no time for congratulations.

Milan began to show signs of recovery and at the same time the Anfield players began to lose their momentum. The game became balanced. The uncertainty of the outcome gripped everyone. Extra time seemed an inevitability. A three all draw would force the compulsory 30 minutes extra time.

And so it did.

Jerzy Dudek and the other Liverpool players celebrate after winning the penalty shoot-out.

INTO EXTRA TIME

The Liverpool players were running on empty tanks; they were exhausted. Lying on the turf they called for help with muscular problems. Gerrard asked for pills as he was suffering from cramp. Nobody was basking in their heroics; there was no time for congratulations; there was concern about lasting the extra thirty minutes, about having enough staying power not to fall apart. The effort they had expended would undoubtedly take its toll.

Even Smicer who had only played in the second half was showing alarming signs of fatigue. Benítez had one planned substitution left, Cissé, who took the place of the exhausted Baros. Milan had one card left and Ancelotti played it by bringing on the powerful Brazilian forward Serginho who came in to attack down the left-hand side. Liverpool's right side needed reinforcement and the job fell to Jamie Carragher who was to show his true professionalism.

Extra time in such a dramatic match took on heroic dimensions. Liverpool kept going as best they could and drew strength from their weakness. Milan had two clear chances. Dudek saved two shots towards the end of extra time. Here was a player whose quality had been so questioned during the season, but whose performance was now keeping his team in the match. There was no doubt that the Polish goalkeeper had saved Liverpool at a critical moment and opened the door to the penalty shoot-out. It was a foretaste of what was to come and in which Dudek was again to play such a central role.

"Don't worry Paco, if we've got this far we're going to win on penalties," Rafa Benítez said to his assistant, Paco Herrera, revealing his state of mind during those anxious moments before the penalty shoot-out. Perhaps he had no time to remember his premonition the night before in front of the hotel lifts when he had predicted what would happen. It was ever closer to coming true. The players could hardly stand; they were shattered.

Now Dudek's time had come.

BETWEEN THE POSTS

Here is where José Manuel Ochotorena, the goalkeeping coach, played a crucial role. At the last minute, just before setting out for Istanbul, he felt the need to study how the Italian team took their penalty kicks. He quickly contacted José Paredes in Orihuela, in the Spanish province of Alicante. Paredes ran a football archive service.

"I need a video of a game in which Milan have been involved in a penalty shoot-out."

The reply was immediate: "The 2003 Champions League final at Old Trafford against Juventus. They won the title on penalties." Ochotorena's response: "Perfect, but I need the tape in Istanbul, by Tuesday at the latest." No sooner said than done, the requested video arrived at its destination in time. Ochotorena passed on all the information that he had gleaned and Dudek received clear and specific instructions on the penalty takers that he would have to face.

Dudek decided that moving about on his goal-line would distract the Milan players. The tactic worked; there was no doubt that his goal-line strategy put off the Italian penalty takers. It was reminiscent of Bruce Grobbelaar and the way he had challenged his opponents in the Rome final of 1984.

The Italians were to go first. Milan started badly with Serginho missing the first shot. Now it was Hamann for Liverpool, and despite having broken a toe during the match he scored. Another Milan penalty. Dudek stopped it. Now Liverpool had a fingerhold on the title. The fans celebrated. Then Cissé. Another goal and an important advantage opened up.

Milan's third shot could have been a turning point. At last they managed to score, as the Swedish striker Tomasson broke their run of misses. Immediately afterwards, Liverpool made their only mistake. The atmosphere in the stadium was electric, emotions were running high. Kaká scored and Milan had hopes of getting back onto level terms in the shoot-out.

Smicer shouldered a heavy responsibilty, if he scored Liverpool would keep their advantage, if he missed they would be level. With sangfroid and with mastery the Czech thudded his shot into the back of the net.

The onus was now back on Milan. They had to score and they had to hope that Liverpool would miss the next one.

Shevchenko, the brilliant Milan star stepped up to the penalty spot. Yet again it was Dudek who was to be the hero.

It was all over. Steven Gerrard, relieved, exhausted and exhilarated, wouldn't need to take his penalty, the fifth.

The Liverpool players formed a tight-knit circle in the centre of the pitch. They hugged each other, their tiredness gone, their bodies driven on by the adrenalin of the moment. Now thousands and thousands of pieces of sparkling glitter exploded into the night air, the stadium erupted with celebration as the fans went wild and Liverpool were crowned the new Champions of Europe.

It had been a battle of immense proportions; indescribable pressure; a memorable comeback and simply extraordinary determination.

They had won a prize that they truly deserved.

On that most beautiful night, Rafa Benítez and his men had reached for the stars.

THE HEROES RETURN

Expectation levels grew by the minute outside the doors of the Crowne Plaza Hotel. It had been a while since the end of the match and most of those present still hadn't taken in what had happened; they couldn't quite believe Liverpool's victory. Security had been stepped up and the Turkish guards zealously controlled all access to the hotel.

Some Spanish journalists had managed to pass themselves off as relatives of the Spanish players, "I'm a relative of Josemi," one had said. Another, as bold as brass, invented a relationship between himself and Luis García. They were very convincing and the local police officers were convinced. In this way at least half a dozen Spanish journalists bluffed their way into the hotel which was now steeped in jubilant chaos.

When Liverpool finally arrived from the Atatürk Stadium after negotiating the fiendish traffic of Istanbul, a guard of honour was formed and the champions were welcomed into the hotel amidst applause and shouts of joy.

Rafa Benítez had already met up with his wife, Montse, who had arrived in Istanbul a few hours before kick-off, on the same flight as those players who hadn't been included in the squad. Back home in Madrid, Rafa's parents followed the match on television. His father, Paco, couldn't control his tears at the final whistle.

As usual, in his moment of triumph, Rafa retained his composure, despite finding himself the centre of attention. He was delighted but it was restrained delight. Afterwards though, his first words to his friends amounted to a confession, an outburst of sincerity. "It was an awful night," he said, before falling into a warm embrace with the pair of them.

The dinner that followed was animated and exuberant. Messages of congratulation were flowing in from everywhere. The atmosphere was euphoric with Rafa responding to endless telephone calls and interview requests. The chants of the Liverpool fans were still ringing in his ears as they called out his name incessantly.

Rafa always does something rather unusual. He has a habit of analysing out loud the incidents in a match and explaining, to whoever is listening, his view of what has happened. That night his mind was still fixed on the game. Outwardly he appeared to be part of the collective celebrations but in his head the images of the match were being replayed. As the ups and downs of that dramatic final hurtled before him, he was scrutinising the details, searching for explanations.

Despite this he wasn't tense. He appeared on several Spanish radio broadcasts and expressed himself elegantly. They, in turn, went out of their way to praise him. Listeners from Spain sent messages of congratulations and their best wishes. He had become greatly admired: the hero of Spanish football. Behind him lay an epic final which he could not stop thinking about.

Before the match he had been more comfortable and less pressured, and he had appeared more decisive. Now in his hour of glory he still wanted to keep to his script, to the role he liked to play. Perhaps it was simply that deep down he was surprised by the success his men had achieved. He was totally open to everyone he talked to that magic night, more than willing to give them his first assessments of the match and to tell them of his concerns. And characteristically, his search for perfection meant that he focused on the things that he hadn't liked rather than wallowing in satisfaction at the enormity of the triumph his team had achieved.

Benítez isn't a man given to complacency and in those moments of success, of glory, he shows that quality more rigorously than ever. He is someone who believes that an exhaustive post-mortem is more constructive than allowing yourself to be swept along with the euphoria. Those who know him well are never too surprised by this reaction; it is what they have come to expect. They encourage him and they express their affection. Rafa Benítez appreciates their warmth and their support, but in his mind he cannot help but replay the match.

It was a long night, finishing well into the early hours. It was almost six o'clock before Rafa Benítez got to bed for the few hours sleep he would get before facing the press conference that had been called for first thing in the morning. And then it would be the journey home.

In front of the press Rafa showed visible signs of tiredness. The event seemed almost a testimonial, with the hangover of a memorable night determining the questions and answers. An air of satisfaction dominated the atmosphere, not the ideal moment for technical analysis or deep readings.

Liverpool had completed an excellent season which had culminated in a success no-one had ever contemplated. Rafa himself was the first to be

European Champions again! The team celebrate Liverpool's fifth European Cup win.

surprised; he hadn't expected to get that far. His plans had been directed at medium and long-term targets, though he had taken advantage of the first opportunity that had come his way.

Now Liverpool awaited them. The party would be enormous. The city was busy preparing for the return of its conquering heroes. Even as the details were being finalised those fortunate supporters who had witnessed the final in person were desperately trying to get home in time. The volume of flights was so high that there was air-traffic congestion.

It was mid-afternoon before the Liverpool team finally arrived at John Lennon Airport. The door of the plane opened to reveal the trophy being held aloft by Steven Gerrard and Rafa Benítez, wearing the club tracksuit and the all red jacket.

From there they went to Melwood where they would climb on board the open-top bus which was to take them on their three-hour journey through the crowded streets of the city. Rafa Benítez was showered with affection and admiration, as the fans chanted his name and sang their version of *La Bamba* in which they'd changed the lyrics to rhyme with his name.

Rafa was deluged with congratulations, including one from Tony Blair, and Cherie Blair, a devoted fan of Liverpool FC.

The city went out of its way to celebrate the return of its champions. Flanked by mounted police, the triumphal procession wove its way through the streets. The huge crowds packed the pavements on both sides. In Lark Hill the procession was almost brought to a standstill by the number of people who had turned out to honour their team.

It was a time of happiness and hope, Liverpool was proud of its champions. Twenty-one years had passed since their last European Cup win. The arrival of the first Spanish manager to English football had brought them luck. Benítez could see just how happy it made people. Now he knew what it meant to represent Liverpool. Now he was one of them.

And so Rafa Benítez has found his ideal club, and now he plans for the future, for his long-term project.

A very special club and a very special manager.

Both were looking for each other.

Now the search is over.

AFTERWORD

NEVER SATISFIED

"The manager is never satisfied."

It's a phrase that many managers have used, and one that sums up the psychological state you enter when you live football from the bench. It perfectly describes the character of Rafa Benítez.

Managers, like Gary Cooper's sheriff in High Noon, are usually alone in the face of danger. Almost everyone watches their every move. They are the weakest link in the chain, the first to break. The players are the first to try to catch them out. They instinctively search for the weak spot in those who give or take away confidence from them and, what's more important, put them in the first team.

Directors behave in a more predictable and basic way. They climb on or off the bandwagon according to the results. If they spot imminent danger they will dispense with their manager's services and look for a replacement. It's not a very original approach.

The press don't come out of it too well either. Some journalists happily make judgments without sufficient knowledge; they don't bother to check their facts, especially those that don't interest them. Managers are easy targets, they can be attacked to satisfy the public, especially when things aren't going well. Some shamelessly sentence their victims before giving them an opportunity to do their work. Having taken their position they won't change their view, no matter what happens. An easy and populist ploy that goes down well. Fans are fickle. They are moved by passionate impulses. Results affect them, and liking or disliking a manager is directly dependent on this.

At the centre of this complex map is the manager; hounded by all these influences – influences which some times converge, but at others pull in opposite directions. It's not easy to be a manager – it's a complicated job, frequently misunderstood. Taking all things into account it brings more heartache than satisfaction. Subjected to enormous pressure, they have little room for manoeuvre. They know it, they're well aware of this reality, they accept the established rules. They have no other option. They are at a disadvantage.

Over 20 years working as a journalist I've had dealings with countless managers. Some famous, others less so, some brought up in the lower divisions, many from other countries. A wide range of managers with different personalities, with their habits, their ideas and also, of course, their odd little ways. There have been all sorts.

The image of the manager has always attracted me because of their position of apparent weakness in this complex world. When they start out they are accorded a generous margin of understanding. For the reasons outlined above, I have tried to understand them. I've seen them suffer and even despair. Many have silently concealed their problems, ignoring the ingratitude that surrounds them. Glory is the exclusive territory of footballers. Moments of jubilation are celebrated by the fans. Vanity is associated with the directors. A manager rarely enjoys his successes, he works to achieve them and offers them to the rest of us, but he has no time to savour his triumphs. He is always thinking about the next fixture, of putting mistakes right, of improving certain aspects. Everything can be made perfect and he finds himself on that continual quest.

An amazing atmosphere of calm prevails.

Rafa Benítez fits this portrait. His insatiable and diligent character keeps him in a constant state of pressure which is passed on to all around him. This has caused him problems and confrontations. Not everybody shares his ideology and to infect others with enthusiasm is an arduous task if someone isn't up for it.

Benítez doesn't usually give way. He is persistent and that obstinacy also creates trouble for him. He is a man of clear ideas and he bases them on hard work, his main commandment. At times of success he is rarely able to fully enjoy it. He doesn't show his feelings which is a tremendous contradiction. After having fought tooth and nail to achieve something, once accomplished, he won't be dragged along by the collective euphoria.

"Benítez arrived at Valencia as a good manager and left as a great manager."

These are the words of Antonio López, his second in command during those three years. He was a fellow student on the coaching course and was on the verge of going with him to Japan at the end of the 90s, attracted by an adventure which in the end didn't materialise. López has had managerial experience in several Spanish clubs but his most famous period was in Bolivia, first alongside Xavier Azkargorta, then on his own. In charge of the country's national team they qualified for the first time for a World Cup, held in the United States in 1994. Azkargorta had been one of their teachers at coaching school, along with Iñaki Sáez, Delgado Meco and the late García Traid amongst others. A teacher who left a profound mark was Santiago Coca, author of a sophisticated book for those who aspire to be coaches, *Hombres para el fútbol* [Men for football]. Antonio López is a thoughtful and well-practised analyst – a discreet man who summed up Benítez's graduation at Mestalla – 'He improved like a good wine until he established his name.' An enriching experience for the manager and for his team of assistants. Three intense and unforgettable years with some hard and difficult moments.

From his very first day at a club, Benítez highlights the importance of having a trusted support team. Being in tune with his colleagues is essential. Their support is vital. At Valencia, López used to watch the first half of matches from the stands. At half-time he would go down to the dressing rooms, exchange opinions with the manager, then stay by his side on the bench during the second half. Benítez is a staunch defender of team work.

He improved like a good wine until he established his name.

Sometimes when is talking, he uses the plural instead of the first person – as a clear indication that the decisions have been agreed with his assistants.

One of his strongest and most recognized virtues is his great facility to adapt to the environment in which he is working. He doesn't take long to get to know the pitfalls and he gets on top of the situation with apparent ease. Despite the badge of office and the triumphs achieved, he always believes there is something that he is missing and seeks tirelessly to broaden his knowledge. He observes and makes deductions, he shuns complacency. His thirst for knowledge is unquenchable.

At the beginning of 1996, after being replaced at Valladolid, he travelled to Italy to learn from established managers. The first visit was to a man he greatly admired, Arrigo Sacchi, creator of the wonderful Milan team, "the best team of all those I've ever seen," Benítez confesses nowadays. At that time Sacchi was managing his country's national side prior to the European Cup in England.

He learnt from the teachers at the coaching school at the Italian Federation premises in Coverziano. He also conversed with other prestigious managers in Italy and carefully studied their training methods. Marcello Lippi was at Juventus, Fabio Capello at Milan and Claudio Ranieri at Fiorentina. He couldn't have suspected at that time that he and Ranieri would cross paths some years later on the Valencia bench.

He could spend a whole day watching football.

After Italy he travelled to England and saw how things operated at several clubs there. That year English football was on the boil with Euro 96 being held there – the first major event since the 1966 World Cup. The great Manchester United were emerging under the leadership of Alex Ferguson, although Newcastle were chasing them for the title. It was a fascinating time with spectacular football being played. Benítez couldn't sit still. His inquisitiveness made him take an interest in all aspects of preparation, he wasn't happy just to watch and listen, he also dared to ask questions, and to discuss ideas, convinced of his own arguments. A long process of learning and assimilation. He could spend a whole day watching football, from first thing in the morning until well into the night – in every division, at every level – always with his inseparable notebook to hand. In time his perseverance paid off. At Valencia the climax of his work came in his third year, with a League and UEFA Cup double, whilst at Liverpool it came in his very first season.

Like all those who stand out, he has his critics who accuse him of a lack of tact in his personal relationships with footballers. Maybe. These are nuances which can be interpreted many ways. A manager and his pupils cannot be friends when they work together as a team. It is a complex situation. This coldness, this distance, is necessary when dealing with players – in a world where football has evolved and with it has come a high degree of professionalisation. In the end though, it does depend on one's perspective.

It's not something that worries the fans too much. When all is said and done there have always been problems in the dressing rooms and there always will be. It's something inherent in the human condition and at the heart of football. A veteran player from Valencia described Alfredo di Stéfano in this way: "Unlike other managers, with Alfredo we would suffer during the week but enjoy ourselves on Sunday, with the others we enjoyed ourselves during the week but died on the pitch on Sundays."

Something similar happens with Benítez. A player knows that he is well managed although there are some aspects that he is not very happy with. The majority of footballers who have been under his command have unanimously shown a reverential respect for his methods and have praised his ability to lead a squad, as well as his skill at thinking about matches and his ability to study opponents.

Benítez lives football with boundless intensity. He's on top of everything and everybody, his sense of responsibility takes him beyond established limits. Some players don't like to accept this control willingly – they don't feel at ease. Others recognise that his criterion of demanding maximum commitment is beneficial for everyone in the long run.

One of the most thoughtful footballers during Benítez's time at Valencia summed it up with insight: "Obsession is good for work, but bad for life." A parallel can be drawn with those basketball trainers, the majority born in the former Yugoslavia, who are so committed to improvement that they force their players to work flat out, with no holding back and no margin for relaxation. They aren't looking for excuses or justifications, they only ask for dedication of body and soul, the maximum amount of work – to give your best at all times.

Rafa's irrepressible desire to use audiovisual material resulted in him producing some educational videos on training methods during his year out before he signed for Tenerife. He worked with Paco Ayestarán, his soulmate. Despite differences in their characters, they understand each other very well. The tapes they made were well received and were seen as being strongly educational. Enamoured by new technology Benítez never hesitates to use it and to benefit from its advantages. On the pitch at Mestalla, Benítez and his colleagues arranged for the installation of cameras to record all the movements of the players during a game. The data gathered enabled him to know their precise movements, the distances travelled, their contribution to the game, all the vital information necessary for him to assess performance objectively – far removed from the subjective impressions which rarely match reality. This was a project guided by a desire for meticulousness, a need for detail which is typical of a researcher.

That's what Benítez is like, that's how he lives football, with a mixture of excessive passion and analytical curiosity. Someone unstintingly dedicated to his profession. A lover of football who has made his vocation the driving force of his whole life.

For further information on our other titles
visit our website

www.dewilewismedia.com